NTC
Vocabulary Builders

Annotated Teacher's Edition

Blue Book

Peter Fisher, Editorial Consultant
National-Louis University

National Textbook Company
a division of *NTC Publishing Group* • Lincolnwood, Illinois USA

NTC Vocabulary Builders

Building Vocabulary the Natural Way

- New words are embedded in strong, carefully crafted contexts that allow students to unlock the meanings independently.

- Consistent emphasis is given to roots and word parts, and their application to English words.

- Reading selections in the humanities, social studies, and sciences parallel the pattern of readings employed in SAT tests while reinforcing cross-curricular learning.

- Focused theme lessons examine words related to a particular area of experience or content, thereby allowing students to differentiate subtle shades of meaning.

- After unlocking the meaning of new words, students immediately apply their knowledge in reading and writing exercises.

- Special features such as "Our Living Language," "Cultural Literacy Note," and "Bonus Word" heighten student interest in words.

- Frequent "Mastering Meaning" features offer a variety of opportunities for using the vocabulary words in realistic writing situations.

- Practical test-taking strategies and practice test questions help students perform well on standardized tests.

- Regular Review and Test pages provide tools for ongoing assessment; four more broadly based tests are included in this Annotated Teacher's Edition.

- Flash cards in each student text give students a convenient means of confirming their hypotheses about the meanings of words, while offering a handy aid for independent review.

Overview of the Program

NTC Vocabulary Builders is a comprehensive vocabulary enrichment series for the secondary school. Its consumable format and instructional strategies are designed to offer you the most effective, yet flexible program available today. The four books that comprise the series are recommended for the grades indicated below. However, individual classrooms vary greatly, and *the highly readable nature of these texts makes them adaptable to other grade levels.*

Red Book ....Grade 9   Green Book ....Grade 11

Blue Book ....Grade 10   Yellow Book ....Grade 12

The Lessons

Each text offers 36 instructional lessons covering a total of 360 words. These words are based on careful examination of adolescent and adult reading material and recent standardized tests. There are three types of lessons:

Context Clues Lessons embed ten words in an interesting and timely essay in one of three curricular areas—humanities, social studies, and sciences. Occurring in a regular cycle, these essays provide strong contexts that allow students to unlock the meaning of the words being studied.

Theme Lessons focus on the vocabulary of specific areas of content or meaning. For example, in the Blue Book students examine the vocabulary of criticism, diplomacy, and art and music.

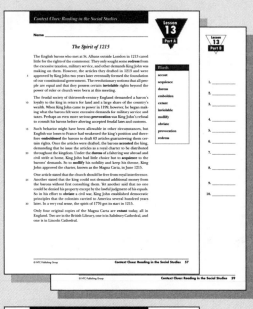

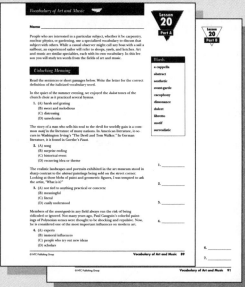

Root Lessons approach words through one or more Latin or Greek roots or word parts. These roots and word parts are the key to understanding not only the words in the lesson, but hundreds of additional English words.

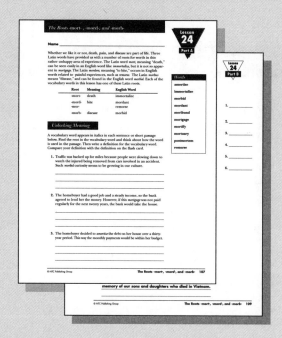

Each lesson consists of two parts, **Part A, Unlocking Meaning,** and **Part B, Applying Meaning.** Each part is printed on a single perforated page to allow easy removal and filing. In addition, individual lessons can be tailored according to the unique needs and pace of your class.

Part A   Unlocking Meaning

The first two pages of each lesson are devoted to helping students learn the meaning of each word on their own. Using context and/or information about roots and word parts, students choose from several proposed definitions, hypothesize about meaning, and confirm their understanding using the flash cards at the back of the book.

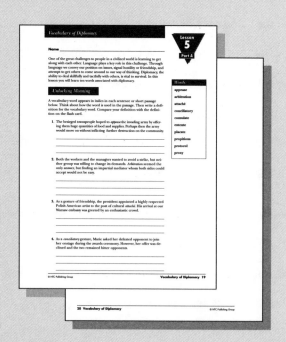

Part B   Applying Meaning

The remaining two pages in each lesson provide opportunities to apply understanding of the words in a reading or writing situation. Each lesson allows students to read and write the words in an original sentence. In this part of the lesson, students are also introduced to appropriate variant forms of the words. For example, students may study the word *indifference* in Part A and be asked to decide whether *indifferent* is used correctly in a sentence in Part B.

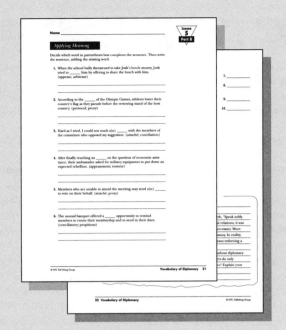

Special Features

Most lessons conclude with one of the following special features designed to heighten interest in words while adding power to the vocabulary.

- **Mastering Meaning** provides opportunities to use the vocabulary words in an original writing assignment. Each Context Clues lesson concludes with this feature.

- **Bonus Word** gives interesting and unusual backgrounds for one or more additional words. These memorable word histories offer easy and practical ways to build vocabulary.

- **Our Living Language** highlights the dynamic nature of our language by focusing on words that have recently entered the language or whose meaning has changed over the years.

- **Cultural Literacy Note** explains terms frequently alluded to in writing that have taken on special meaning.

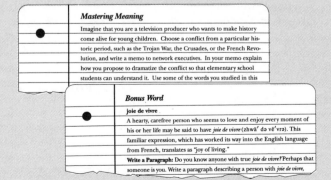

Mastering Meaning

Imagine that you are a television producer who wants to make history come alive for young children. Choose a conflict from a particular historic period, such as the Trojan War, the Crusades, or the French Revolution, and write a memo to network executives. In your memo explain how you propose to dramatize the conflict so that elementary school students can understand it. Use some of the words you studied in this

Bonus Word

joie de vivre

A hearty, carefree person who seems to love and enjoy every moment of his or her life may be said to have *joie de vivre* (zhwä' də vē'vrə). This familiar expression, which has worked its way into the English language from French, translates as "joy of living."

Write a Paragraph: Do you know anyone with true *joie de vivre?* Perhaps that someone is you. Write a paragraph describing a person with *joie de vivre*,

Our Living Language

noblesse oblige

The concepts of democracy and equality were almost unknown in the Middle Ages. Instead of authority rising from the consent of the people, it was thought to flow down from God through the king and the nobility. Being born to high rank, however, did carry with it a certain "obligation" to look after the commoners and peasants. This was not so much from a

Cultural Literacy Note

red herring

Red herring are fish that have a strong odor when they are cured by salting. The odor is so strong, in fact, that if a red herring is dragged across the trail of an animal being chased by hunting dogs, the dogs will become confused and begin following the trail of the herring. Consequently, *red herring* has come to refer to any deliberate distraction, especially in an argument. Calling someone a socialist in a debate over

Teaching and Learning Aids

Test-Taking Strategies

Each text includes four sections designed to help students take standardized tests. Covering a wide variety of formats such as antonyms, reading comprehension, analogies, and standard English usage, these lessons familiarize students with test configurations and offer valuable suggestions for approaching each test and avoiding common pitfalls.

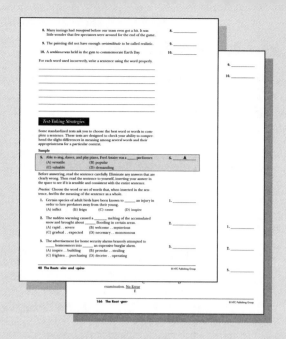

Review and Test

Following every third lesson is a two-page test covering the words in the three previous lessons. Employing standardized testing formats, these tests can be used as self-correcting reviews or as an evaluation tool. In addition, this Annotated Teacher's Edition includes four more tests, each covering nine lessons, or one quarter of the book. Because these tests appear only in the Annotated Teacher's Edition, you can choose when to distribute them.

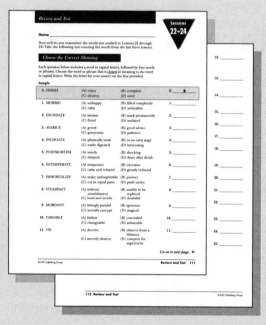

Flash Cards

A flash card for every vocabulary word presented in the book is included at the back of each student text. Each flash card is identified by lesson and includes the pronunciation, definition, and any derived forms studied in the lesson. Students may remove these cards and use them to review word meanings or to check their understanding.

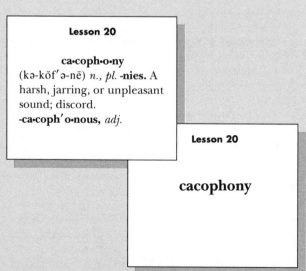

Assessment Record

Name _____ Class _____

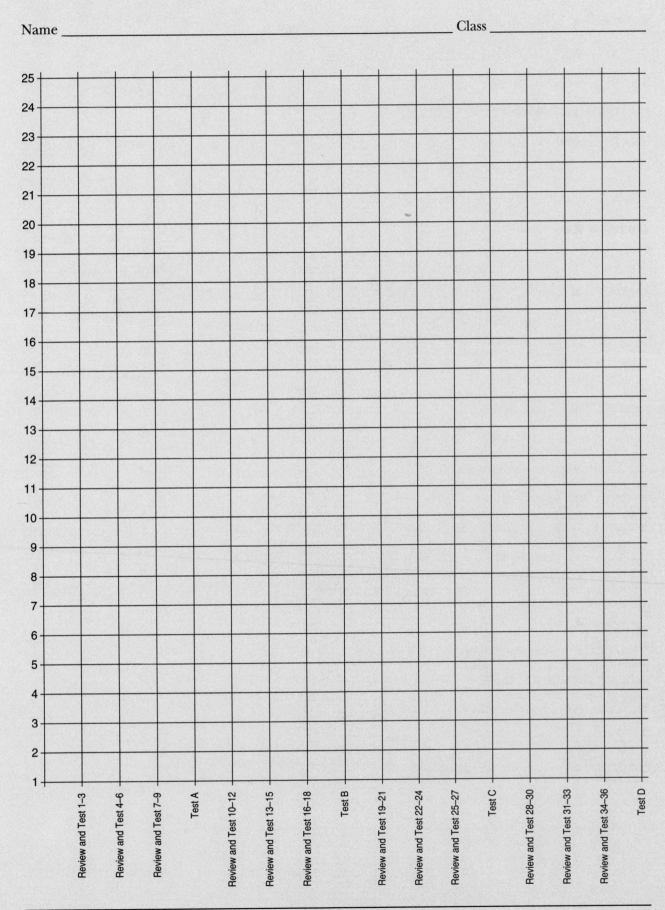

25
24
23
22
21
20
19
18
17
16
15
14
13
12
11
10
9
8
7
6
5
4
3
2
1

Review and Test 1–3
Review and Test 4–6
Review and Test 7–9
Test A
Review and Test 10–12
Review and Test 13–15
Review and Test 16–18
Test B
Review and Test 19–21
Review and Test 22–24
Review and Test 25–27
Test C
Review and Test 28–30
Review and Test 31–33
Review and Test 34–36
Test D

Periodic Tests

Answer Key

Test A	*Test B*	*Test C*	*Test D*
1. C	1. D	1. E	1. D
2. A	2. A	2. A	2. C
3. B	3. E	3. A	3. B
4. E	4. B	4. D	4. A
5. B	5. C	5. C	5. E
6. D	6. C	6. D	6. C
7. A	7. A	7. E	7. A
8. D	8. D	8. B	8. B
9. E	9. B	9. C	9. D
10. C	10. B	10. D	10. A
11. C	11. C	11. C	11. C
12. A	12. A	12. A	12. E
13. B	13. E	13. E	13. E
14. D	14. D	14. B	14. A
15. D	15. A	15. B	15. B
16. B	16. g	16. d	16. d
17. E	17. d	17. f	17. a
18. C	18. a	18. j	18. i
19. A	19. f	19. b	19. h
20. D	20. h	20. c	20. f
21. B	21. e	21. h	21. c
22. A	22. c	22. g	22. e
23. D	23. i	23. i	23. b
24. E	24. j	24. a	24. j
25. B	25. b	25. e	25. g

Part 1

Decide which definition best fits the italicized word in the sentence. Write the letter for your choice on the answer line.

1. The player's *adroit* movements frustrated his opponents and eventually led to victory for his team.

    (A) unpredictable   (B) unusual   (C) skillful   (D) familiar   (E) famous

    1. _____

2. The movie star's *unpretentious* manner came as a surprise to her adoring fans.

    (A) modest   (B) exaggerated   (C) proud   (D) conceited   (E) clumsy

    2. _____

3. After inspecting the aircraft, the flight engineer announced that he had not discovered any *egregious* mechanical problems.

    (A) complicated   (B) conspicuously bad   (C) easily corrected

    (D) careless   (E) life-threatening

    3. _____

4. Hearing his name called, Darren seemed *incredulous* as he rose and walked to the stage.

    (A) proud   (B) expressionless   (C) confused

    (D) overjoyed   (E) disbelieving

    4. _____

5. Mounting sales of bicycles seemed to *augur* a profitable year for retailers of sports clothing.

    (A) encourage   (B) foretell   (C) prevent   (D) increase   (E) allow

    5. _____

6. Helen is one of the most *ingenuous* people I have ever observed.

    (A) clever   (B) dull and boring   (C) talkative

    (D) naive and simple   (E) intelligent

    6. _____

7. The senior advisor suggested that the company take a more *judicious* approach to the problem.

    (A) sensible   (B) aggressive   (C) secret   (D) legal   (E) public

    7. _____

8. After a hard-fought campaign, you might expect the candidates to exchange a few *conciliatory* remarks.

    (A) hostile   (B) humorous   (C) carefully worded

    (D) soothing   (E) outrageous

    8. _____

9. Even when things were going very badly for him, Shane maintained the *semblance* of self-confidence.

    (A) deception   (B) similarity   (C) simplicity

    (D) hypocrisy   (E) appearance

    9. _____

10. The counselor advised us not to be upset by the *foibles* of those around us.

    (A) insensitive remarks   (B) moral differences

    (C) minor weaknesses   (D) superior manner   (E) physical appearance

    10. _____

Go on to next page. ➤

Each question below includes a word in capital letters, followed by five words or phrases. Choose the word or phrase that is <u>closest</u> in meaning to the word in capital letters. Write the letter for your answer on the line provided.

11. CONDESCENDING   (A) moving downward   (B) carefully designed   11._____
(C) acting superior   (D) crafty
(E) honest and sincere

12. STARK   (A) harsh   (B) bird-like   12._____
(C) firmly secured   (D) unforgivable   (E) damaged

13. HONE   (A) ignore   (B) sharpen   (C) clean out   13._____
(D) send out   (E) advise

14. COVERT   (A) convert   (B) exposed   (C) admired   14._____
(D) secret   (E) poisonous

15. WASPISH   (A) colorful   (B) painful   (C) illegal   15._____
(D) irritable   (E) stained

16. PALATABLE   (A) royally attired   (B) agreeable to the taste   16._____
(C) easily shaped   (D) tightly packed   (E) portable

17. CIRCUMSCRIBE   (A) professional writer   (B) speak directly   17._____
(C) mix together   (D) meet by chance   (E) limit

18. FLOUNDER   (A) sink   (B) swim gracefully   (C) move awkwardly   18._____
(D) one who begins a business   (E) profanity

19. NOXIOUS   (A) offensive   (B) sudden   (C) smooth   19._____
(D) mismatched   (E) flexible

20. IRREPRESSIBLE   (A) wrinkled   (B) difficult to reverse   20._____
(C) struggling   (D) uncontrollable   (E) dull

21. SIMULATE   (A) inspire   (B) imitate   21._____
(C) encourage   (D) confuse   (E) surrender

22. LEGACY   (A) something inherited   (B) legal action   22._____
(C) wealth   (D) solemn promise
(E) punishment

23. POMPOUS   (A) expanded   (B) specialist   23._____
(C) ceremonious   (D) conceited   (E) explosive

24. NUANCE   (A) recent event   (B) energy   24._____
(C) quiet sound   (D) numeral
(E) subtle quality

25. PROTOCOL   (A) early example   (B) custom   25._____
(C) tiny organism   (D) formal announcement
(E) trusted advisor

Part 1 Choose the Correct Meaning

Each question below includes a word in capital letters, followed by five words or phrases. Choose the word or phrase that is <u>closest</u> in meaning to the word in capital letters. Write the letter for your answer on the line provided.

1. OVERT   (A) avoid   (B) hidden   1. _____
       (C) concealed   (D) straightforward
       (E) dishonest

2. FAUX PAS   (A) small blunder   (B) glorious victory   2. _____
       (C) unpleasant odor   (D) unclear message
       (E) established plan of action

3. SUPERFLUOUS   (A) exceptional   (B) flowing together   3. _____
       (C) strong   (D) changeable   (E) unnecessary

4. INFLUX   (A) bend   (B) steady inward flow   (C) influence   4. _____
       (D) friendly behavior   (D) threat

5. ACCOST   (A) determine the value of   (B) activate   (C) confront   5. _____
       (D) accuse   (E) make calm

6. INVIOLABLE   (A) expensive   (B) unobtainable   6. _____
       (C) untouchable   (D) violated   (E) required

7. ADULTERATE   (A) contaminate   (B) mature   7. _____
       (C) act immorally   (D) filter   (E) prohibit

8. PERIPHERY   (A) preference   (B) loyal followers   8. _____
       (C) part of a building   (D) outermost region
       (E) attractive appearance

9. PERVASIVE   (A) slippery   (B) spread throughout   (C) convincing   9. _____
       (D) rare   (E) highly offensive

10. INNUENDO   (A) immediate repetition   (B) sly suggestion   10. _____
       (C) interruption   (D) secret plot
       (E) acknowledgment

11. DERIDE   (A) halt   (B) praise excessively   (C) ridicule   11. _____
       (D) recognize   (E) move from place to place quickly

12. LOQUACIOUS   (A) talkative   (B) sickly   12. _____
       (C) overly critical   (D) pleasant-sounding   (E) elegant

13. UPBRAID   (A) uproot   (B) rearrange   (C) support   13. _____
       (D) dispose of   (E) denounce

Go on to next page. ➤

14. EUTHANASIA   (A) distant continent   (B) extreme happiness   **14.** _____
                           (C) imitation   (D) mercy killing   (E) type of speech

15. RAIL   (A) complain bitterly   (B) mislead   **15.** _____
                           (C) explain carefully   (D) make strong or solid
                           (E) exaggerate

Part 2 Matching Words and Meanings

Match the definition in Column B with the word in Column A.
Write the letter for your choice on the answer line.

Column A	Column B	
16. dense	a. existent	**16.** _____
17. intrinsic	b. mild, indirect term	**17.** _____
18. extant	c. prevent	**18.** _____
19. duress	d. essential	**19.** _____
20. eclectic	e. make better	**20.** _____
21. ameliorate	f. threat of force	**21.** _____
22. obviate	g. thick	**22.** _____
23. nouveau riche	h. made up from mixed sources	**23.** _____
24. gambol	i. newly wealthy	**24.** _____
25. euphemism	j. run playfully	**25.** _____

Part 1 Choose the Correct Meaning

Each question below includes a word in capital letters, followed by five words or phrases. Choose the word or phrase that is <u>closest</u> in meaning to the word in capital letters. Write the letter for your answer on the line provided.

1. INDELIBLE   (A) grateful   (B) annoying   **1.** _____
                       (C) delicate   (D) ruined   (E) permanent

2. AVARICE   (A) desire for great wealth   (B) dislike   **2.** _____
                       (C) unattractive habit   (D) stinginess
                       (E) tendency to eat or drink too much

3. HERESY   (A) opinion that is contrary to accepted beliefs   **3.** _____
                       (B) disagreeable remark   (C) religious belief
                       (D) illogical argument   (E) unsupported statement

4. DULCET   (A) carpenter's tool   (B) obstacle   (C) quarrelsome   **4.** _____
                       (D) sweet and mellow   (E) object of ridicule

5. AVOCATION   (A) support   (B) charitable activity   **5.** _____
                       (C) something done for pleasure   (D) careless remark
                       (E) detailed instructions

6. REMORSE   (A) repeat unnecessarily   (B) cancel   **6.** _____
                       (C) coordinated movement   (D) sorrow   (E) recognize

7. MORBID   (A) musical   (B) immoral   (C) formed from the earth   **7.** _____
                       (D) curious   (E) gloomy

8. VOUCH   (A) type of document   (B) give assurances   **8.** _____
                       (C) send away   (D) argue against
                       (E) a solemn oath

9. VIE   (A) observe secretly   (B) fill with life   (C) compete   **9.** _____
                       (D) pardon   (E) permit

10. PARSIMONY   (A) money paid to a former spouse   (B) serious crime **10.** _____
                       (C) reckless behavior   (D) stinginess   (E) popularity

11. OBSOLETE   (A) sleek in appearance   (B) destroyed   (C) outdated   **11.** _____
                       (D) modern   (E) unwelcome

12. WANE   (A) decrease   (B) grow in size   (C) predict   **12.** _____
                       (D) snare   (E) remove forcibly

13. CATACLYSM   (A) official pardon   (B) celebration   **13.** _____
                       (C) amusing incident   (D) interrogation
                       (E) violent disturbance

Go on to next page. ➤

14. NOTORIOUS   (A) disguised   (B) well-known for evil acts   14. _____
                    (C) noticeable   (D) twisted
                    (E) sufficient for one's needs

15. EDIFICE   (A) statue   (B) building   (C) food   15. _____
                  (D) farmland   (E) container used for storage

Part 2 Matching Words and Meanings

Match the definition in Column B with the word in Column A.
Write the letter for your choice on the answer line.

Column A	Column B	
16. stagnate	a. tendency	16. _____
17. improvise	b. greed	17. _____
18. carnivore	c. fresh and unspoiled	18. _____
19. rapacity	d. become motionless	19. _____
20. pristine	e. suitable for farming	20. _____
21. equivocate	f. perform without preparation	21. _____
22. immortalize	g. give eternal life to	22. _____
23. avant-garde	h. avoid taking a clear position	23. _____
24. proclivity	i. people trying new ideas	24. _____
25. arable	j. meat eater	25. _____

Name _____

Part 1 Choose the Correct Meaning

Each question below includes a word in capital letters, followed by five words or phrases. Choose the word or phrase that is <u>closest</u> in meaning to the word in capital letters. Write the letter for your answer on the line provided.

1. MALLEABLE   (A) disagreeable   (B) wicked   (C) immovable   1. _____
(D) easily formed or influenced   (E) limited

2. IMPLAUSIBLE   (A) continuous   (B) impossible   (C) unlikely   2. _____
(D) desirable   (E) insulting

3. URBANITE   (A) rare mineral   (B) resident of a city   3. _____
(C) highly refined person   (D) declining neighborhood
(E) heavily populated

4. VICTUAL   (A) food   (B) essential   4. _____
(C) unfortunate victim   (D) lively personality   (E) utensil

5. SALUTARY   (A) speech given at graduation   (B) enclosure for animals   5. _____
(C) sanitary   (D) skillful in use of the hands   (E) beneficial

6. BELIE   (A) believe   (B) restrain   (C) contradict   6. _____
(D) reject without hesitation   (E) call out

7. PERNICIOUS   (A) harmful   (B) suspicious   (C) periodic   7. _____
(D) lasting indefinitely   (E) stimulating

8. COMPULSORY   (A) difficult   (B) required   8. _____
(C) composed of many elements   (D) throbbing
(E) done without thinking

9. EPHEMERAL   (A) lengthy   (B) disorganized   (C) unimportant   9. _____
(D) lasting a short time   (E) worldly

10. INVETERATE   (A) firmly established   (B) low form of animal life   10. _____
(C) inexperienced   (D) studious   (E) unusual

11. DISPEL   (A) confuse   (B) rush forth   (C) drive away   11. _____
(D) gather together   (E) save from ruin

12. RELINQUISH   (A) value highly   (B) modify   (C) cause great suffering   12. _____
(D) reminder of the past   (E) let go

13. NEOPHYTE   (A) prehistoric   (B) easily ignited   (C) expert   13. _____
(D) diplomat   (E) beginner

14. ABATE   (A) lessen   (B) return with interest   14. _____
(C) argue formally   (D) assist   (E) carry off

15. CULL   (A) type of sea bird   (B) pick out   (C) gently calm   15. _____
(D) insult   (E) bind together

Go on to next page. ➤

Part 2 Matching Words and Meanings

Match the definition in Column B with the word in Column A.
Write the letter for your choice on the answer line.

Column A	Column B	
16. impede	a. practical; workable	16._____
17. viable	b. honesty and integrity	17._____
18. volatile	c. polite in behavior and manner	18._____
19. desultory	d. block	19._____
20. apogee	e. genuine	20._____
21. urbane	f. farthest or highest point	21._____
22. bona fide	g. safeguard	22._____
23. probity	h. lacking order or organization	23._____
24. immutable	i. given to sudden changes	24._____
25. bulwark	j. not subject to change	25._____

NTC
Vocabulary Builders

Blue Book

Peter Fisher, Editorial Consultant
National-Louis University

National Textbook Company
NTC a division of *NTC Publishing Group* • Lincolnwood, Illinois USA

Acknowledgments

The pronunciation key used in the flash cards has been reprinted by permission from the AMERICAN HERITAGE DICTIONARY OF THE ENGLISH LANGUAGE, THIRD EDITION, copyright © 1992 by Houghton Mifflin Company.

Cover Illustration: Sandie Burton
Cover Design: Ophelia Chambliss
Editorial Development: Cottage Communications

Published by National Textbook Company, a division of NTC Publishing Group.

Library of Congress Catalog Card Number: 94-65414

4 5 6 7 8 9 0 VL 9 8 7 6 5 4 3 2 1

Contents

Name _____

Master of the Wordless Theater

Schooled in the **nuances** of gesture and facial expression, mimes encourage audiences to examine body movements with the **keen** attention of a detective searching for clues. The body language of mimes unravels the mysteries of character, motivation, and plot that they **adroitly**
5 crowd into sketches lasting only minutes. The truly skilled, like Marcel Marceau, invite us to share a world that exists only in the imagination.

Born in France, Marcel Marceau developed an early taste for pantomime as he watched the antics of Charlie Chaplin, Buster Keaton, and the Marx Brothers in movies that broke down language barriers and
10 national differences. After serving in the army during World War II, he entered the School of Dramatic Art in Paris. There he created his famous character Bip, who was named after the character Pip in Charles Dickens's *Great Expectations*.

Marceau tells most of his stories through this simple, pathetic, and
15 **irrepressible** clown. In a stovepipe hat decorated with a bobbing red flower, Bip walks against the imaginary wind, nurses a seemingly sore finger, pulls an imaginary rope in a tug-of-war, catches a make-believe butterfly, and climbs an imaginary flight of stairs. His performances are deceptively simple, yet they **embody** the most intricate theatrical tech-
20 niques. With his body as his primary instrument, he twists, turns, and bends. His eyes and his **stark**, almost shocking, painted-white face further absorb the audience in the action. As Marceau has said, "Pantomime is the art of expressing feelings and attitudes, not a means of expressing words through gestures."

25 Marcel Marceau's aim is simply to make his audience see, feel, and hear the invisible. Each of the sketches in his **repertoire** offers a glimpse into the amusing **foibles** of human nature. With posture and facial expression alone, he re-creates **fugitive** displays of misery, jealousy, solitude, defeat, frustration, and shame.

30 Having given some 15,000 performances in more than 100 countries, Marceau now devotes most of his energy to the students enrolled in his mime school and troupe. A great believer in technique, he drills them in classical and modern dance, juggling, fencing, acrobatics, and jazz in addition to the grammar of mime. These young artists are his **legacy**.
35 Through them, he hopes to introduce the magic of mime to a generation shaped by the noise and action of television.

Words
adroit
embody
foible
fugitive
irrepressible
keen
legacy
nuance
repertoire
stark

Each word in this lesson's word list appears in dark type in the selection you just read. Think about how the vocabulary word is used in the selection, then write the letter for the best answer to each question.

1. Which words could best replace *nuances* in line 1?
   (A) embarrassing repetition (B) loud outcries
   (C) legal obligations (D) slight variations

   1. _____ **D** _____

2. Which word could best replace *keen* in line 2?
   (A) intense (B) struggling
   (C) broken (D) voluntary

   2. _____ **A** _____

3. Which word or words could best replace *adroitly* in line 4?
   (A) mindlessly (B) skillfully and cleverly
   (C) authoritatively (D) foolishly

   3. _____ **B** _____

4. Which word or words could best replace *irrepressible* in line 15?
   (A) easily frightened (B) capable of being provoked
   (C) overpowering (D) impossible to restrain

   4. _____ **D** _____

5. Which word or words could best replace *embody* in line 19?
   (A) give definite form to (B) slyly manipulate
   (C) discard (D) authorize

   5. _____ **A** _____

6. Which word or words could best replace *stark* in line 21?
   (A) twisted (B) thin
   (C) harsh (D) barely noticeable

   6. _____ **C** _____

7. A *repertoire* (line 26) can best be explained as ____.
   (A) background (B) forceful devotion to a
   specific cause
   (C) a formal promise (D) the pieces or parts a player or
   group is prepared to perform

   7. _____ **D** _____

8. *Foibles* (line 27) can best be explained as ____.
   (A) serious errors produced (B) minor, excusable weaknesses
   by carelessness in character
   (C) short tales accompanied (D) disregard of danger
   by morals

   8. _____ **B** _____

9. Which word or words could best replace *fugitive* in line 28?
   (A) difficult to watch (B) unnecessary
   (C) lasting only a short time (D) criminally negligent

   9. _____ **C** _____

10. A *legacy* (line 34) can best be explained as ____.
    (A) a constructive habit (B) a reassuring declaration
    (C) something handed down (D) something provided by
    from one generation to agreement
    another

    10. _____ **C** _____

Applying Meaning

Each question below contains a vocabulary word from this lesson.
Answer each question "yes" or "no" in the space provided.

1. Would an *irrepressible* horse be the appropriate mount for an inexperienced rider?

2. Is there a *stark* contrast between granite cliffs and soft foliage?

3. Can perfume have a *fugitive* fragrance?

4. Is an *adroit* person awkward and clumsy?

5. Does a person who understands the *nuances* of a subject comprehend only its basic elements?

1. _____ **no** _____

2. _____ **yes** _____

3. _____ **yes** _____

4. _____ **no** _____

5. _____ **no** _____

For each question you answered "no," write a sentence using the vocabulary word correctly.

Answers will vary.

_____

_____

_____

_____

_____

_____

_____

_____

_____

_____

_____

Decide which word in parentheses best completes the sentence. Then write the sentence, adding the missing word.

6. Her habit of eating with her fingers was a(n) _____ that Jenny worked hard to change. (embodiment; foible)

foible _____

_____

_____

7. Dad was disappointed that "Misty" was not part of the jazz pianist's
   _____. (legacy; repertoire)

   repertoire _____

   _____

   _____

8. For patriotic individuals, the flag is the _____ of the spirit and character of their country. (embodiment; nuance)

   embodiment _____

   _____

   _____

9. Arching her back and hissing, the mother cat was _____ aware of the
   new owners who had come to claim her babies. (adroitly; keenly)

   keenly _____

   _____

   _____

10. Freedom of speech is just one of the _____ of the framers of the
    Constitution. (foibles; legacies)

    legacies _____

    _____

    _____

Mastering Meaning

Superstars—outstanding actors, musicians, and athletes—are capable of doing things that other people only dream about. Whether they have natural ability, skill cultivated through practice, or both, these people often function as inspirations for others. Select a famous person whose talents you respect and admire and do some research into the person's background. Then write a report explaining why this person is a super-star. Use some of the words you studied in this lesson.

Name _____

Attitude can be defined as a state of mind or feeling with regard to some matter. Your attitude, and how you show it, have a strong impact on everything you do. Being positive or negative will not only affect how you act, but it will also determine how others react to you. The words in this lesson describe ten types of attitudes and outlooks you might have yourself or encounter in others.

Unlocking Meaning

Read the sentences or short passages below. Write the letter for the correct definition of the italicized vocabulary word.

According to the late science fiction writer Isaac Asimov, people are *arrogant* if they believe that they are the only intelligent life in the universe.

1. (A) not in conformity with law
   (B) overly convinced of their own importance
   (C) common in a particular locality
   (D) lacking healthy diets

Commuters may ignore the homeless in bus and train stations. This *cavalier* blindness makes their daily journey more bearable.

2. (A) characterized by confusion
   (B) arousing fear or awe
   (C) lacking validity
   (D) unconcerned with important matters

Having grudgingly agreed to visit the creative writing class, the famous author offered only *condescending* comments about the work of the amateur writers.

3. (A) characterized by a superior manner
   (B) worthy of worship
   (C) devout or religious
   (D) marked by a smooth, lyrical style

At the end of the Trojan War, Achilles was *contemptuous* of his rivals. He illustrated his negative attitude by dragging the body of Hector, his slain enemy, around the walls of Troy.

4. (A) somewhat fearful
   (B) overcome by embarrassment
   (C) earthy and uncomplicated
   (D) filled with scorn

Words
arrogant
cavalier
condescending
contemptuous
ebullient
egocentric
haughty
pompous
unpretentious
waspish

1. _____**B**_____

2. _____**D**_____

3. _____**A**_____

4. _____**D**_____

It had not snowed for nearly nine months, so when the snow finally fell on the mountains, hundreds of *ebullient* skiers headed for the slopes.

5. (A) frightened
   (B) persistent
   (C) enthusiastic
   (D) exhausted

5. _____ **C** _____

Rhett Butler left Scarlett O'Hara at the end of *Gone with the Wind*. Among other complaints, he felt he could no longer tolerate her *egocentric* neglect of others' feelings. It seemed she thought only of herself.

6. (A) self-centered
   (B) supportive
   (C) distracted
   (D) bewildered

6. _____ **A** _____

Haughty and uncooperative, the star performer treated the rest of the actors as if they were amateurs. He eventually was removed from the cast of the play because of his depressing effect on morale.

7. (A) using few words
   (B) overly proud and vain
   (C) resistant to work
   (D) capable of moving with ease

7. _____ **B** _____

Mary, Queen of Scots, placed self-interest ahead of her country's needs when she claimed that the throne of England was rightfully hers. As a result of her *pompous* actions, Queen Mary lost her head in addition to her throne.

8. (A) having an evil influence
   (B) clearly apparent
   (C) generous
   (D) too proud of one's importance

8. _____ **D** _____

The *unpretentious* bungalow sat amidst impressive mansions. Although their house was small and humble, the family was very proud of it.

9. (A) modest
   (B) desirable
   (C) run-down
   (D) realistic

9. _____ **A** _____

Tired and *waspish*, the car salesman made several impatient remarks to browsers. He later regretted these comments when the customers refused to buy a car from him.

10. (A) calm
    (B) off-balance
    (C) bad-tempered
    (D) perplexed

10. _____ **C** _____

Applying Meaning

Each question below contains a vocabulary word from this lesson. Answer each question "yes" or "no" in the space provided.

1. Would an *ebullient* child sit quietly for long periods of time?

     1. _____ **no** _____

2. Might an *unpretentious* person own two or three expensive cars?

     2. _____ **no** _____

3. Would a *pompous* individual be quick to tell you that he had been invited to the governor's inauguration?

     3. _____ **yes** _____

4. Would an *egocentric* sports star want to talk about himself and his success?

     4. _____ **yes** _____

5. Might a *condescending* person believe that those who are less fortunate deserve what they get?

     5. _____ **yes** _____

6. Would a voter support a candidate with a *cavalier* attitude toward unemployment and the economy in his district?

     6. _____ **no** _____

For each question you answered "no," write a sentence using the vocabulary word correctly.

Answers will vary.

_____

_____

_____

_____

_____

_____

_____

_____

_____

Write each sentence below. In the space write a form of the word in parentheses. The form of the word in parentheses may be correct.

7. Captain Ahab's _____ was so great that he swore he would strike the sun if it insulted him. (arrogant)

arrogance _____

_____

_____

8. With her nose in the air, the wealthy lawyer obviously could not see the puddle; drenched feet were the reward for her _____. (haughty)

haughtiness

_____

_____

9. "I'll get there when I can," Joanna snarled _____. (waspish)

waspishly

_____

_____

10. Once viewed with _____ by art critics, the paintings of the French impressionists are among the most valuable works of art in the world today. (contemptuous)

contemptuousness or contempt

_____

_____

Our Living Language

Waspish, which means "easily irritated or annoyed," undoubtedly took its name from the insect that stings anyone who disturbs it. Many other adjectives used to describe people also came from animal names. For example, the word *bovine* can be applied to a person who resembles an ox, a cow, or a similar animal. Bovine individuals tend to be sluggish and dull, like the animals of the genus *Bos*.

Cooperative Learning: With a group of classmates, brainstorm a list of animals that have given rise to words describing how people act, such as *crabby* and *slothful*. Make a dictionary of such terms by including a possible word history, a definition, and a short paragraph characterizing the type of person to whom the word applies. You might also consider including animal-based phrases that describe people's actions, such as *to monkey around*.

Lesson
3
Part A

Name _____

The root *-greg-* comes from the Latin word *grex*, meaning "herd" or "flock." The root *-junct-* comes from the Latin word *jungere*, which means "to join." When combined with different prefixes and suffixes, these roots give us a number of words that share the idea of coming together. For example, a *conjunction* connects words, phrases, clauses, or sentences, while a *congregation* is a gathering of people or things. In this lesson, you will learn other words with one of these roots.

Root	Meaning	English Word
-greg-	flock, herd	aggregate
-junct-	join	adjunct
-join-		enjoin
-jun-		junta

Words

- adjunct
- aggregate
- congregate
- egregious
- enjoin
- gregarious
- injunction
- juncture
- junta
- segregate

Unlocking Meaning

Write the vocabulary word that fits each clue below. Then say the word and write a short definition. Compare your definition and pronunciation with those given on the flash card.

1. If you were the president of a country, you would not like seeing these military officers "join" together. They would probably want to replace you.

junta. Definitions will vary. _____

_____

_____

2. This four-syllable adjective could describe someone who enjoys being with a "herd" of other people.

gregarious. Definitions will vary. _____

_____

_____

3. This word begins with the Latin prefix *ad-*, meaning "to" or "toward." Add this meaning to the meaning of the root.

adjunct. Definitions will vary. _____

_____

_____

4. It is difficult to find the "herd" in this adjective. It came into English through the Latin word *egregius*, meaning "outstanding." You might say that the word now means "outstanding for the wrong reasons."

egregious. Definitions will vary.

_____

_____

5. This "join" verb begins with the prefix *en-*. You could try to do this to someone who plays loud music in the middle of the night.

enjoin. Definitions will vary.

_____

_____

6. This word came from the Latin *segregare*, meaning "to group apart."

segregate. Definitions will vary.

_____

_____

7. This word begins with *ag-*, a form of the Latin prefix *ad-*. It can be a noun, a verb, or an adjective. The word *total* is one synonym.

aggregate. Definitions will vary.

_____

_____

8. You sometimes read of courts issuing one of these to stop something. Unlike the answer to number 5, this noun begins with the prefix *in-*.

injunction. Definitions will vary.

_____

_____

9. This word combines the *con-* prefix, meaning "together," with the "flock" root. Add the meanings of the two parts.

congregate. Definitions will vary.

_____

_____

10. This noun refers to the place where two things join together.

juncture. Definitions will vary.

_____

_____

_____

Applying Meaning

Read each sentence below. Write "correct" on the answer line if the vocabulary word has been used correctly. Write "incorrect" on the answer line if the vocabulary word has been used incorrectly.

1. The *gregarious* Chin family enjoys having company for dinner and taking group vacations.

    1.   **correct**

2. The *adjunct* of the two highways needed a traffic signal very badly.

    2.   **incorrect**

3. Members of the ruling *junta* were often seen carrying guns.

    3.   **correct**

4. Her *egregious* piece of writing received a high grade because of its well-defended ideas and its vivid examples.

    4.   **incorrect**

5. The bus driver *enjoined* the policeman from giving him a ticket.

    5.   **incorrect**

For each word used incorrectly, write a sentence using the word properly.

Answers will vary.

_____

_____

_____

_____

_____

_____

_____

_____

Decide which word in parentheses best completes the sentence. Then write the sentence, adding the missing word.

6. Vietnamese food is a subtle _____ of French and Asian influences that combines meat or fish with vegetables. (aggregate; congregation)

    aggregate _____

_____

_____

7. A court _____ prohibited the Olympic Committee from holding its disciplinary hearing until after the games. (injunction; juncture)

    injunction _____

_____

_____

8. To prevent others from catching the highly contagious virus, those afflicted were _____ in separate hospital wards. (congregated; segregated)

segregated

9. The _____ of students in the courtyard was disturbing the classes that were still in session. (aggregation; congregation)

congregation

10. The problem with the rocket occurred at a very important _____ during liftoff. (junta; juncture)

juncture

Our Living Language

Herd and *flock* are just two of the many words used to describe groupings of animals. Some other common terms include *pack, covey, swarm, colony, school,* and *drove.* Whole books have been devoted to the creation of terms to describe animals and their groupings. For example, the lark's song is so beautiful that it produces an intense feeling of elation in its listeners. This may be why a flight of larks is called an exaltation of larks.

Cooperative Learning: Work with a partner to brainstorm some characteristics for the groups of people listed below. Then, based on these characteristics, decide on a suitable term for a group of them. Try to stay away from ordinary or existing terms, such as a gang of teenagers or a league of ballplayers.

teenagers	teachers
business executives	parents
athletes	senior citizens

Name _____

How well do you remember the words you studied in Lessons 1 through 3?
Take the following test covering the words from the last three lessons.

Part 1 Choose the Correct Meaning

Each question below includes a word in capital letters, followed by four words
or phrases. Choose the word or phrase that is <u>closest</u> in meaning to the word
in capital letters. Write the letter for your answer on the line provided.

Sample

S. FINISH	(A) enjoy	(B) complete	**S.**	**B**
	(C) destroy	(D) enlarge		

1. POMPOUS	(A) self-important	(B) ceremonious	1.	**A**
	(C) formal	(D) outstanding		
2. ADJUNCT	(A) wise	(B) subordinate	2.	**B**
	(C) released	(D) highly prized		
3. SEGREGATE	(A) deny	(B) insult	3.	**C**
	(C) separate	(D) combine		
4. KEEN	(A) clever	(B) blunt	4.	**D**
	(C) simple	(D) intense		
5. WASPISH	(A) sensitive	(B) easily irritated	5.	**B**
	(C) protective	(D) dangerous		
6. ADROIT	(A) awkward	(B) uninformed	6.	**C**
	(C) skillful	(D) unfamiliar		
7. FOIBLE	(A) small fault	(B) clever trick	7.	**A**
	(C) official command	(D) carefree attitude		
8. NUANCE	(A) soft noise	(B) subtle quality	8.	**B**
	(C) something fresh or new	(D) argument		
9. EGOCENTRIC	(A) self-centered	(B) circular	9.	**A**
	(C) attractive	(D) enclosed		
10. JUNCTURE	(A) prohibition	(B) worthless items	10.	**C**
	(C) intersection	(D) military rulers		

Go on to next page. ➤

11. CONTEMPTUOUS	(A) full of disdain (C) skillful	(B) modern (D) short-tempered	11. ___A___
12. STARK	(A) endangered (C) impulsive	(B) light and filmy (D) absolute	12. ___D___
13. AGGREGATE	(A) aggravate (C) explain	(B) gathered together (D) rearrange	13. ___B___
14. INJUNCTION	(A) command (C) foreign interference	(B) crossroads (D) type of injury	14. ___A___
15. CONGREGATE	(A) welcome (C) assemble	(B) exclude from membership (D) separate into groups	15. ___C___

Part 2 Matching Words and Meanings

Match the definition in Column B with the word in Column A.
Write the letter of the correct definition on the line provided.

Column A	Column B	
16. cavalier	a. something handed down	16. ___b___
17. gregarious	b. showing offhand disregard	17. ___f___
18. enjoin	c. impossible to hold back	18. ___d___
19. unpretentious	d. prohibit	19. ___g___
20. ebullient	e. displaying a sense of superiority	20. ___h___
21. egregious	f. enjoying the company of others	21. ___i___
22. repertoire	g. simple and modest	22. ___j___
23. legacy	h. enthusiastic	23. ___a___
24. irrepressible	i. extremely bad	24. ___c___
25. condescending	j. pieces or parts a person or group is ready to perform	25. ___e___

Name _____

The Code Talkers

During World War II, an exceptional group of Americans **honed** speech into a precise weapon and went to war for the United States. Despite the fact that they participated in battles from Guadalcanal to Okinawa, their story is at best a footnote in war **archives**. They were the Navajo code talk-
5 ers, and theirs remains one of the few unbroken codes in military history.

Unknown to the enemy and most Americans, Native Americans had served **covertly** as communication specialists in World War I by sending messages in their tribal languages. Their use was **circumscribed**, however, by their lack of words for such crucial terms as *machine gun* and *grenade*. When
10 World War II broke out, a young man who had grown up on a reservation proposed a guaranteed-unbreakable code to the Marines. The officers at Camp Elliott were **incredulous** at first, but when Philip Johnston and fif- teen Navajo friends demonstrated their **facility** with the system, the Marines made a decision that would influence the outcome of the war.

15 Previous warfare codes had been too easily broken by the enemy. Germans deciphering English codes could tap common linguistic roots. Japanese soldiers eavesdropping on radio broadcasts were often gradu- ates of American universities. Navajo, however, was entirely foreign to the enemy. It is a tonal language, so its vowels rise and fall, changing mean-
20 ing with pitch. A single Navajo verb can translate into an entire English sentence. The Marines were confident that the **arcane** language would give them the needed edge.

To devise their vocabulary, the Navajo code talkers named planes after birds, and ships after fish. When they ran out of flora and fauna, they con-
25 structed word games: *district* became the Navajo words for *deer ice strict* and *belong* became *long bee*. Within days, the Navajo **polyglots** were encoding and decoding sensitive military **dispatches** quickly and almost effortlessly.

More than 3,600 Navajos served in World War II, but only 420 were code talkers. Members of all six Marine Corps divisions in the Asian-Pacific the-
30 ater, they **surmounted** the difficulties and baffled the Japanese for three years with a hodgepodge of everyday Navajo and some 400 code words of their own creation. Although many of the Navajo code talkers remained in the Marines and served in Korea and Vietnam, the top secret code was never used again. It was declassified in 1968. Only then did the secret
35 come out.

Words

arcane

archives

circumscribe

covert

dispatch

facility

hone

incredulous

polyglot

surmount

Each word in this lesson's word list appears in dark type in the selection you just read. Think about how the vocabulary word is used in the selection, then write the letter for the best answer to each question.

1. Which word could best replace *honed* in line 1?
   (A) discarded   (B) neutralized
   (C) sharpened   (D) domesticated

   1. _____ **C** _____

2. *Archives* (line 4) can best be explained as _____.
   (A) historical records   (B) branches of knowledge
   (C) descriptions of battle (D) treaties between enemies
       techniques

   2. _____ **A** _____

3. Which word could best replace *covertly* in line 7?
   (A) occasionally   (B) reluctantly
   (C) ineffectively   (D) secretly

   3. _____ **D** _____

4. Which word could best replace *circumscribed* in line 8?
   (A) avoided   (B) limited
   (C) extended   (D) respected

   4. _____ **B** _____

5. *Incredulous* (line 12) can best be described as _____.
   (A) showing doubt or disbelief (B) pulled in opposite directions
   (C) agitated with anxiety   (D) showing good judgment

   5. _____ **A** _____

6. Which word or words could best replace *facility* in line 13?
   (A) lack of logical sequence   (B) inconsistency
   (C) aptitude or skill   (D) lack of familiarity

   6. _____ **C** _____

7. Something that is *arcane* (line 21) can best be explained as _____.
   (A) old before its time   (B) passing quickly
   (C) understood by only a few   (D) unrealistic

   7. _____ **C** _____

8. Which words could best replace *polyglots* in line 26?
   (A) fortune tellers   (B) people with knowledge of several
                                       languages
   (C) people with little   (D) people who move from place
       education   to place

   8. _____ **B** _____

9. *Dispatches* (line 27) can best be explained as _____.
   (A) official communications   (B) sources of irritation
   (C) newspapers   (D) equipment

   9. _____ **A** _____

10. Which word could best replace *surmounted* in line 30?
    (A) proclaimed   (B) withheld
    (C) removed   (D) overcame

    10. _____ **D** _____

Applying Meaning

Follow the directions below to write a sentence using a vocabulary word.

1. Describe the effect that not knowing how to read or write might have on a person. Use the word *circumscribe* or one of its related forms.

   Sample Answer: Not knowing how to read or write would seriously circumscribe one's ability to get a good job.

2. Describe a specialized subject that few people are familiar with. Use the word *arcane*.

   Sample Answer: Griffin's thesis covered the arcane topic of Parthian military tactics.

3. Describe someone who tries to disguise or hide his or her boredom. Use the word *covert* or one of its related forms.

   Sample Answer: As her uncle loaded the sixth tape of home movies into the VCR, Denise stretched and yawned covertly.

4. Describe a famous person who has faced some difficult challenges. Use the word *surmount* or one of its related forms.

   Sample Answer: Both Pete Gray and Jim Abbott surmounted the lack of an arm to become major league baseball players.

5. Describe a city or nation where people of many nationalities live. Use the word *polyglot*.

   Sample Answer: Chicago is a polyglot city where English, Polish, and Spanish are frequently heard on the street.

6. Describe how a foreign correspondent for a newspaper might handle some important news. Use the word *dispatch*.

   Sample Answer: After the announcement, the correspondent sent an urgent dispatch to his editor.

Write each sentence below. In the space write a form of the word in parentheses. The form of the word in parentheses may be correct.

7. Gilda blinked _____ behind her diving mask as she gazed at the wreckage of a fifteenth-century Spanish galleon. (incredulous)

    incredulously

8. I wonder if Ann Landers has an _____ who organizes letters by subject matter. Any time a reader asks for a reprint of a letter, the advice columnist seems to be able to provide it. (archives)

    archivist

9. _____ the stick by patiently rubbing it against a boulder, the hungry camper tried to make a spear so he could catch a mountain trout for lunch. (hone)

    Honing

10. After she injured her hand, physical therapy improved Ingrid's _____ in manipulating small objects. (facility)

    facility

Mastering Meaning

Imagine that you are a television producer who wants to make history come alive for young children. Choose a conflict from a particular historic period, such as the Trojan War, the Crusades, or the French Revolution, and write a memo to network executives. In your memo explain how you propose to dramatize the conflict so that elementary school students can understand it. Use some of the words you studied in this lesson.

Name _____

One of the great challenges to people in a civilized world is learning to get along with each other. Language plays a key role in this challenge. Through language we convey our position on issues, signal hostility or friendship, and attempt to get others to come around to our way of thinking. Diplomacy, the ability to deal skillfully and tactfully with others, is vital to survival. In this lesson you will learn ten words associated with diplomacy.

Unlocking Meaning

A vocabulary word appears in italics in each sentence or short passage below. Think about how the word is used in the passage. Then write a definition for the vocabulary word. Compare your definition with the definition on the flash card.

1. The besieged townspeople hoped to *appease* the invading army by offering them huge quantities of food and supplies. Perhaps then the army would move on without inflicting further destruction on the community.
   Definitions will vary.
   _____
   _____

2. Both the workers and the managers wanted to avoid a strike, but neither group was willing to change its demands. *Arbitration* seemed the only answer, but finding an impartial mediator whom both sides could accept would not be easy.
   Definitions will vary.
   _____
   _____

3. As a gesture of friendship, the president appointed a highly respected Polish American artist to the post of cultural *attaché*. His arrival at our Warsaw embassy was greeted by an enthusiastic crowd.
   Definitions will vary.
   _____
   _____

4. As a *conciliatory* gesture, Marie asked her defeated opponent to join her onstage during the awards ceremony. However, her offer was declined and the two remained bitter opponents.
   Definitions will vary.
   _____
   _____

Words
appease
arbitration
attaché
conciliatory
consulate
entente
placate
propitious
protocol
proxy

5. The United States opened a *consulate* in the new nation immediately after the results of the disputed election were announced. This clearly signaled American approval of the new president.

   Definitions will vary.

   _____

   _____

6. After months of negotiations, England and France reached an economic *entente*. In return for England's shipments of North Sea oil, France would reduce its tariffs on other English imports.

   Definitions will vary.

   _____

   _____

7. Ernest felt he should have been given the leading role in the play. So in an attempt to *placate* him, the director offered to make him her special assistant.

   Definitions will vary.

   _____

   _____

8. It would not be easy asking the coach to resign. It might be wise to wait for a *propitious* moment, such as after the next humiliating loss.

   Definitions will vary.

   _____

   _____

9. Attempting to shake hands with Queen Elizabeth is a serious violation of *protocol*. No one is permitted to touch the British monarch.

   Definitions will vary.

   _____

   _____

10. Unable to attend the ceremonial signing of the agreement, the president sent the secretary of state as his official *proxy*.

    Definitions will vary.

    _____

    _____

Name _____

Lesson
5
Part B

Applying Meaning

Decide which word in parentheses best completes the sentence. Then write the sentence, adding the missing word.

1. When the school bully threatened to take Josh's lunch money, Josh tried to _____ him by offering to share the lunch with him. (appease; arbitrate)

   appease _____

   _____

2. According to the _____ of the Olympic Games, athletes lower their country's flag as they parade before the reviewing stand of the host country. (protocol; proxy)

   protocol _____

   _____

3. Hard as I tried, I could not reach a(n) _____ with the members of the committee who opposed my suggestion. (attaché; conciliation)

   conciliation _____

   _____

4. After finally reaching an _____ on the question of economic assistance, their ambassador asked for military equipment to put down an expected rebellion. (appeasement; entente)

   entente _____

   _____

5. Members who are unable to attend the meeting may send a(n) _____ to vote on their behalf. (attaché; proxy)

   proxy _____

   _____

6. The annual banquet offered a _____ opportunity to remind members to renew their membership and to send in their dues. (conciliatory; propitious)

   propitious _____

   _____

Each question below contains at least one vocabulary word from this lesson. Answer each question "yes" or "no" in the space provided.

7. Would you expect to find an *attaché* in a *consulate?*

7. _____ **yes** _____

8. Would your sister's best friend be the best person to *arbitrate* an argument you are having with your sister?

8. _____ **no** _____

9. Could you *placate* an angry dog by poking it with a stick?

9. _____ **no** _____

10. Should a diplomat honor his host's *protocol* when paying an official visit to the Japanese *consulate?*

10. _____ **yes** _____

For each question you answered "no," write a sentence using the vocabulary words correctly.

Answers will vary.

Bonus Words

gunboat diplomacy

President Theodore Roosevelt often quoted the proverb, "Speak softly and carry a big stick." It suggested that in international relations, it was wise to be cautious but to be prepared to use force if necessary. More recently this philosophy has been labeled *gunboat diplomacy.* In reality, gunboat diplomacy is no diplomacy at all. It simply means enforcing a foreign policy through military threats or actions.

Write a Paragraph: Can you think of an example of gunboat diplomacy in daily life? For example, are there things you or others do only because there is an expressed or implied threat of force? Explain your example in a paragraph.

Lesson
6
Part A

Name _____

The Latin word *judicare* means "to judge." It appears as *-jud-* in a number of modern English words. A similar Latin word, *jurare*, means "to swear" in the sense of making a solemn pledge. The *-jur-* root you see in words like *perjury* comes from this Latin word. The Greek word for "people" is *demos*. It appears as part of many English words such as *democracy*. Look for these roots and word parts in this lesson's words.

Root	Meaning	English Word
-jud-	to judge	judicious
-jur-	to swear	conjure perjure
-demo- -dem-	people	demographics demagogue

Unlocking Meaning

A vocabulary word appears in italics in each sentence or short passage below. Find the root in each vocabulary word and choose the letter for the correct definition. Write the letter for your choice on the answer line.

1. The doctors urged the people of the island to *abjure* their belief in witchcraft and evil curses and take the shots they needed to avoid an epidemic.

   (A) advertise   (B) explain carefully
   (C) solemnly renounce (D) practice

2. The dispute between Missouri and Illinois over the ownership of an island in the Mississippi River had to be *adjudicated* in a federal court.

   (A) settled through   (B) repeatedly ignored
       judicial procedure
   (C) put on display   (D) sold

3. It is interesting how names affect us. Iceland *conjures* up the image of a frozen wasteland, while Greenland makes one think of lush land-scapes. In reality, neither image is accurate.

   (A) humiliates   (B) brings to mind
   (C) argues persuasively (D) turns away

4. After years of poverty and international disapproval, the country was ripe for a *demagogue* to seek power by blaming all the nation's prob-lems on some religious or ethnic minority.

   (A) leader who appeals to (B) outlawed political party
       emotion or prejudice
   (C) religious person   (D) great leader

Words

abjure

adjudicate

conjure

demagogue

demographics

endemic

judicious

jurisdiction

jurisprudence

perjure

1. _____**C**_____

2. _____**A**_____

3. _____**B**_____

4. _____**A**_____

5. The *demographics* indicated that Middletown was a perfect place to test the new product. Its diverse population was a cross-section of the entire country.

   (A) local politicians   (B) newspaper article
   (C) strange pictures   (D) characteristics of a population

   5. _____ **D** _____

6. Certain diseases such as hemophilia are *endemic* to the royal families of Europe, probably the result of generations of intermarriage.

   (A) desirable   (B) rare; unusual
   (C) sole possession   (D) peculiar to certain people or places

   6. _____ **D** _____

7. With so many things to do during final exam week, Paul had to make *judicious* decisions about how he used his time.

   (A) legal   (B) controversial
   (C) wise   (D) simple

   7. _____ **C** _____

8. The lawyer argued that the judge had no right to try the case because the alleged crime took place outside the *jurisdiction* of the local court.

   (A) area of legal authority (B) vision or view
   (C) land owned by the   (D) knowledge or influence
       government

   8. _____ **A** _____

9. She was always fascinated by *jurisprudence.* It is little wonder that she finished law school at the top of the class.

   (A) young people   (B) the science of law
   (C) virtuous behavior   (D) common sense

   9. _____ **B** _____

10. Rather than *perjure* himself by contradicting his earlier statement, the witness refused to answer any questions when the lawyer cross-examined him.

    (A) boast   (B) tell a lie under oath
    (C) honor   (D) amuse

    10. _____ **B** _____

Applying Meaning

Follow the directions below to write a sentence using a vocabulary word.

1. Write about a decision you or someone you know made. Use any form of the word *judicious*.

   Sample Answer: With her limited amount of money,

   Alicia had to choose judiciously from the items on the

   grocery store's shelves.

2. Recall a place you visited or an event you attended. Write about the associations you have with that place or event. Use the word *conjure*.

   Sample Answer: When I recall my trip to Hawaii,

   I conjure up images of palm trees and blue surf.

3. Describe the people of a community or nation. Use any form of the word *demographics*.

   Sample Answer: According to some experts, by the year

   2050 the demographics of the United States will include

   a high percentage of people over 65 years of age.

4. Use the word *endemic* to tell about a disease or illness that affects people living in certain places.

   Sample Answer: Malaria is endemic to people living in

   hot, humid climates such as that of Central America,

   because mosquitoes thrive in such climates.

5. Write about a belief or practice you or someone you know once held but have since given up. Use any form of the word *abjure*.

   Sample Answer: By the time I reached the age of seven,

   I had abjured my belief in Santa Claus.

6. Describe the responsibilities of a judge or law enforcement official. Use the word *jurisdiction*.

   Sample Answer: Unlike local police officers, the sheriff

   has jurisdiction over the entire county.

Read each sentence or short passage below. Write "correct" on the answer line if the vocabulary word has been used correctly. Write "incorrect" on the answer line if the vocabulary word has been used incorrectly..

7. In our world history class we learned about the many gods and *demagogues* of the early religions.

7. **incorrect**

8. The court refused to *adjudicate* the case because the accused had not been advised of his rights.

8. **correct**

9. The British system of *jurisprudence* is based largely on a tradition of common laws. The United States, however, has the Constitution as the basis of its laws.

9. **correct**

10. After gaining control of the government, the dictator attempted to *perjure* his opposition by having them secretly tried and imprisoned.

10. **incorrect**

For each word used incorrectly, write a sentence using the word properly.

Answers will vary.

_____

_____

_____

_____

_____

_____

_____

_____

_____

_____

Bonus Word

Machiavellian

Niccolo Machiavelli (1469-1527) was an Italian political philosopher.

His most famous book, *The Prince,* advised rulers to rely on fear, not

love, as the strategy for gaining and holding power. He even went so

far as to advise lying, deceit, and other forms of treachery if neces-

sary. Using this practical but unethical tactic is now referred to as

Machiavellian, a term sometimes applied to corrupt or unscrupulous

politicians or authorities.

Complete the Statement: What kinds of activities might a Machiavel-

lian engage in? See how many ways you can complete this statement:

"You know a politician is a Machiavellian when . . . ."

Name _____

4-6

How well do you remember the words you studied in Lessons 4 through 6? Take the following test covering the words from the last three lessons.

Part 1 Antonyms

Each question below includes a word in capital letters, followed by four words or phrases. Choose the word or phrase that is most nearly <u>opposite</u> in meaning to the word in capital letters. Consider all choices before deciding on your answer. Write the letter for your answer on the line provided.

Sample

S. SLOW	(A) lazy (C) fast	(B) simple (D) common	S. **C**
1. JUDICIOUS	(A) legal (C) foolish	(B) pious (D) complicated	1. **C**
2. SURMOUNT	(A) overcome (C) trample	(B) surrender (D) betray	2. **B**
3. INCREDULOUS	(A) convinced (C) ordinary	(B) incredible (D) hateful	3. **A**
4. COVERT	(A) silent (C) unnecessary	(B) covered (D) obvious	4. **D**
5. ARCANE	(A) well-known (C) modern	(B) old-fashioned (D) useless	5. **A**
6. CONCILIATORY	(A) pleasant (C) individual	(B) hostile (D) forgotten	6. **B**
7. ENTENTE	(A) intentional (C) argument	(B) narrow (D) exit	7. **C**
8. ABJURE	(A) judge (C) delay	(B) discard (D) accept	8. **D**
9. CIRCUMSCRIBE	(A) erase completely (C) remove limitations	(B) mark permanently (D) record	9. **C**
10. CONJURE	(A) trick (C) act illegally	(B) suppress (D) soothe	10. **B**

Go on to next page. ➤

11. PROPITIOUS   (A) unfortunate   (B) obvious   11. _____A_____
                  (C) thrifty   (D) dishonored

12. ENDEMIC   (A) easily understood   (B) universal 12. _____B_____
                  (C) serious   (D) pleasant

13. APPEASE   (A) satisfy   (B) embrace   13. _____D_____
                  (C) misbehave   (D) anger

14. FACILITY   (A) dishonesty   (B) excitement   14. _____C_____
                  (C) lack of ability (D) ease

15. HONE   (A) cast out   (B) plead   15. _____C_____
                  (C) blunt   (D) resign

Part 2 Matching Words and Meanings

Match the definition in Column B with the word in Column A.
Write the letter of the correct definition on the line provided.

Column A	Column B		
16. archives	a. to lie under oath	16.	i
17. protocol	b. to settle in court	17.	c
18. jurisdiction	c. the etiquette of diplomacy	18.	f
19. attaché	d. made of many languages	19.	g
20. perjure	e. substitute	20.	a
21. dispatch	f. range of authority	21.	j
22. polyglot	g. type of diplomat	22.	d
23. adjudicate	h. to calm	23.	b
24. placate	i. place for storing historic papers	24.	h
25. proxy	j. official message or report	25.	e

Name _____

The Free Spirits of the Molecular World

Matter comes in three forms—solid, liquid, and gas. Of the three, gas has been the most useful to scientists. In fact, it was Robert Boyle's work with gases around 1660 that **augured** the science of chemistry some two hundred years later. Boyle found that the volume of a gas decreases as pres-
5 sure is applied to it, provided that temperature and other factors remain constant. In other words, if you squeeze a gas harder, it gets smaller. Moreover, the relationship between pressure and volume can be predicted quite exactly. If you double the pressure, the volume is reduced by half. Gases, it seems, are the free spirits of the molecular world, wandering
10 around as they please unless confined.

About one hundred years later, French chemist Jacques Charles proposed that the volume of a gas is directly related to its temperature, provided the pressure remains the same. In this case, however, the volume of a gas increases as the temperature is increased.

15 In the early 1800s John Dalton, an English chemist, used the work of Boyle, Charles, and a **bevy** of others to propose a theory that all matter is made up of atoms and molecules. This theory signaled the beginning of the science of chemistry. Dalton defined an atom as the smallest particle of an element. An atom of oxygen, for example, is represented by the
20 letter O in H_2O, the formula for water. It is the smallest particle that has all the characteristics of oxygen. However, oxygen does not exist natural-ly as a single atom. In the atmosphere, two such atoms are linked one be-hind the other as a **tandem** molecule, symbolized by the formula O_2.

Evidence that gases are free-moving molecules, **careening** around us,
25 becomes apparent whenever something spicy is cooking, as odor is the most common method for detecting many gases. Baking bread, for example, releases millions of gaseous molecules into the air. Because these gases tend to move from areas of high concentration, say the kitchen, to areas of low concentration, like the living room, the odor spreads like a **gossamer** fog.
30 Before long, the entire neighborhood knows that a **palatable** treat is being prepared in your kitchen.

While advertising your choice of **cuisine** may not appeal to you, several industries depend on this property of gases. The effectiveness of perfume or air fresheners in combating **noxious** odors depends on these wander-
35 ing gas molecules. Gas also plays a role in the generation of light. Travel down any main street after dark and your eyes are **assaulted** by numerous, **iridescent** signs. These colorful displays are the result of a gas, usually neon, being energized by an electrical current.

Words

- assault
- augur
- bevy
- careen
- cuisine
- gossamer
- iridescent
- noxious
- palatable
- tandem

40

Unlocking Meaning

Each word in this lesson's word list appears in dark type in the selection you just read. Think about how the vocabulary word is used in the selection, then write the letter for the best answer to each question.

1. Which word could best replace *augured* in line 3?
   (A) confused
   (B) replaced
   (C) foreshadowed
   (D) demanded

   1. _____ **C** _____

2. Which word or words could best replace *bevy* in line 16?
   (A) group
   (B) misunderstanding
   (C) ancestor
   (D) military unit

   2. _____ **A** _____

3. In line 23, *tandem* means _____.
   (A) two together
   (B) bitter
   (C) lightly colored
   (D) invisible

   3. _____ **A** _____

4. Which word could best replace *careening* in line 24?
   (A) fighting
   (B) whistling
   (C) crawling
   (D) lurching

   4. _____ **D** _____

5. In line 29, *gossamer* means _____.
   (A) surprising
   (B) light and filmy
   (C) demanding
   (D) heavenly

   5. _____ **B** _____

6. Which word could best replace *palatable* in line 30?
   (A) awful
   (B) friendly
   (C) tasty
   (D) sour

   6. _____ **C** _____

7. In line 32, *cuisine* means _____.
   (A) relatives
   (B) pleasure
   (C) type of food
   (D) travel plans

   7. _____ **C** _____

8. In line 34, *noxious* means _____.
   (A) distasteful
   (B) beautiful
   (C) noisy
   (D) warm

   8. _____ **A** _____

9. In line 36, *assaulted* means _____.
   (A) destroyed
   (B) deceived
   (C) reversed
   (D) attacked

   9. _____ **D** _____

10. Which word or words could best replace *iridescent* in line 37?
    (A) dull
    (B) rainbow-colored
    (C) simple
    (D) confusing

    10. _____ **B** _____

Applying Meaning

Follow the directions below to write a sentence using a vocabulary word.

1. Make a prediction about the weather based on something you notice. Use any form of the word *augur*.

   Sample Answer: The dark sky and sudden wind do not augur well for tomorrow's weather.

2. Describe the scene outside a theater before a sold-out performance by a popular rock musician or band. Use the word *bevy*.

   Sample Answer: A bevy of excited fans crowded in front of the theater before the performance.

3. Describe any appropriate object using the word *gossamer*.

   Sample Answer: The sun streamed through gossamer clouds as it slowly sank to the horizon.

4. Describe any appropriate object or sensation using the word *noxious*.

   Sample Answer: The factory ruined the river by dumping noxious chemicals into it.

5. Describe an ice skater. Use any form of the word *careen*.

   Sample Answer: The inexperienced skater careened off the side of the rink and into another skater.

Read each sentence or short passage below. Write "correct" on the answer line if the vocabulary word has been used correctly. Write "incorrect" on the answer line if the vocabulary word has been used incorrectly.

6. The new restaurant features several varieties of Mexican *cuisine*.

6. ___correct___

7. Her *iridescent* behavior was an embarrassment to everyone who knew her.

7. ___incorrect___

8. The teacher agreed not to *assault* any homework over the spring vacation.

8.   **incorrect**

9. The citizens had mixed feelings about the chemical plant. They needed the jobs the plant offered, but they could hardly stand the *noxious* fumes it produced.

9.   **correct**

10. The soup was quite tasteless, but the cook was reluctant to make it more *palatable* by adding salt.

10.   **correct**

11. The spoiled child threw a temper *tandem* in the store when his mother refused to buy him some candy.

11.   **incorrect**

12. High on a hill we could see a *bevy* of wild turkeys resting in the shade of a large oak tree.

12.   **correct**

For each word used incorrectly, write a sentence using the word properly.

Answers will vary.

_____

_____

_____

_____

_____

_____

_____

_____

_____

_____

_____

_____

_____

_____

Mastering Meaning

Describe the sensory experiences you might have in a good restaurant as you watch meal after meal being served. What sights, smells, and sounds would you pick up? Use some words you studied in this lesson.

Lesson 8 Part A

Name _____

Some English words look or sound alike or have similar meanings. They are easy to confuse in reading or writing situations. Consequently, special attention needs to be devoted to their meaning and use. The words in this lesson consist of word pairs that are easily confused. By studying these word pairs, you can eliminate this confusion.

Unlocking Meaning

A vocabulary word appears in italics in each sentence or short passage below. Think about how the word is used in the passage. Then write a definition for the vocabulary word. Compare your definition with the definition on the flash card.

Words
adverse
averse
flounder
founder
ingenious
ingenuous
persecute
prosecute
precede
proceed

1. The manufacturers claimed the plane could fly under even the most *adverse* weather conditions. It had proven itself in snow, sleet, and hurricane-force winds.

   Definitions will vary. _____

   _____

   _____

2. The candidate was *averse* to debating her opponent on television. Since she already held a huge lead according to the opinion polls, she felt she had nothing to gain and everything to lose.

   Definitions will vary. _____

   _____

   _____

3. As we moved through the drifting snow, Buster and I *floundered* along as best we could. I slid into a fence and held on to it tightly until I could regain my balance. Buster's claws scratched helplessly on the ice before all four legs slid out from under him.

   Definitions will vary. _____

   _____

   _____

4. As the water rushed through the gash in the hull, the passengers scrambled for the lifeboats. It was only a matter of time before the ship *foundered* in the icy water.

   Definitions will vary. _____

   _____

   _____

5. My mechanic had an *ingenious* solution to the problem. Instead of discarding the worn tire, he suggested we make it the spare tire and use it briefly and only in emergencies.

Definitions will vary.

_____

_____

_____

6. We all had to smile at his *ingenuous* behavior at the party. He actually asked the hostess how much she paid for her gown and how much money she earned last year.

Definitions will vary.

_____

_____

_____

7. The Nazi efforts to *persecute* the Jews have been well documented, from the time Jewish shops were closed down to the eventual imprisonment and execution of millions of Jews in forced labor camps.

Definitions will vary.

_____

_____

_____

8. The decision to *prosecute* the suspect was delayed until witnesses were found, evidence was evaluated, and conviction seemed certain.

Definitions will vary.

_____

_____

_____

9. A thorough study of existing laws and past court decisions must *precede* any effort to amend the Constitution. If we fail to perform this first step, all other efforts might be wasted.

Definitions will vary.

_____

_____

_____

10. The dentist had to wait for the painkillers to numb the affected area before she could *proceed* to work on the tooth.

Definitions will vary.

_____

_____

_____

Name _____

Applying Meaning

Decide which word in parentheses best completes the sentence. Then write the sentence, adding the missing word.

1. The architect is known for his ____ skyscrapers. His recent work features colorful windows scattered throughout each floor. (ingenious; ingenuous)

   ingenious
   _____
   _____

2. The noisy party in the next apartment created an _____ environment for completing my mathematics homework. (adverse; averse)

   adverse
   _____
   _____

3. Tradition requires that cabinet officers _____ diplomats when entering the legislative chambers. (precede; proceed)

   precede
   _____
   _____

4. Thanks to a system of pumps and watertight chambers, the designer insisted that the ship could not possibly ____ regardless of the damage a collision might cause. (flounder; founder)

   founder
   _____
   _____

5. Since the exam was scheduled for early the next morning, I was ____ to staying up late in order to watch television. (adverse; averse)

   averse
   _____
   _____

6. As an outspoken critic of the mayor, Ms. Inez felt she was being ____ when her car was ticketed, her property taxes were raised, and her street was left unrepaired. (persecuted; prosecuted)

   persecuted
   _____
   _____

7. With sand underfoot and a heavy load on his back, the soldier _____ across the island in search of his regiment. (floundered; foundered)

floundered

_____

_____

8. Jeff may have appeared foolish when he asked the head waiter to bring him a hot dog, but there was something about his ____ nature that made everyone like him. (ingenious; ingenuous)

ingenuous

_____

_____

9. At the border the customs agent searched our automobile and luggage. After a few minutes, he told us to ____ . (precede; proceed)

proceed

_____

_____

10. The newspaper's editorial urged the attorney general to ____ anyone involved in the demonstration. The editorial claimed that the entire event was just an excuse for vandalism. (persecute; prosecute)

prosecute

_____

_____

Our Living Language

flounder¹, flounder²

In the dictionary there are two entries for *flounder*. They have two distinct meanings and two separate histories, but they are pronounced and spelled the same way. These words are called *homographs*. (The second meaning of *flounder* is a type of fish.) Most dictionaries provide separate entries for homographs and number each entry with a small raised number. This distinguishes them from words with multiple definitions.

Use an Unabridged Dictionary: Check the meaning and history of these homographs: date¹, date²; lie¹, lie²; pry¹, pry²; graft¹, graft²; fry¹, fry².

Name _____

The Latin word *similis* means "like." It came into English as the root *-sim-* or *-sem-* through the French word *similaire*. These roots still carry part of the original Latin meaning as well as a more general meaning of "sameness" or "togetherness." One of the most interesting roots in modern English is *-spire-*. It comes from the Latin word *spirare*, meaning "to breathe." However, because of the belief that ideas, and even life itself, were "breathed" into one, this root has a variety of meanings in English words.

Root	Meaning	English Word
-sim- -sem-	like, same	simulate ensemble
-spire- -spir- -pir-	to breathe	inspiration aspirant expiration

Unlocking Meaning

A vocabulary word appears in italics in each sentence or short passage below. Find the root or word part in the vocabulary word and choose the letter for the correct definition. Write the letter for your choice on the answer line.

1. Several eager, young *aspirants* tried out for the leading role in the film. Each wanted desperately to become a Hollywood star.
   (A) immigrants
   (B) people trying to achieve a position or goal
   (C) distant relatives
   (D) converts to a particular religion

   1. ___**B**___

2. Because of its location between North America and the Far East, Hawaii has had to *assimilate* many different cultures.
   (A) reject; discard
   (B) absorb; make similar
   (C) examine
   (D) ignore

   2. ___**B**___

3. In addition to her fashionable new dress, her *ensemble* included a red leather belt, a matching pair of boots, and a wide-brimmed hat with a red band.
   (A) something made up of harmonious parts
   (B) hostile or proud attitude
   (C) social position
   (D) useless or cheap possessions

   3. ___**A**___

   4. ___**D**___

4. Unfortunately, the accident occurred after the *expiration* of the insurance policy. As a result, Beth must pay for the damage to the automobile.
   (A) destruction
   (B) evaluation
   (C) beginning or start of something
   (D) close or end of something

Words

aspirant

assimilate

ensemble

expiration

inspiration

semblance

simile

simulate

transpire

verisimilitude

---

5. The athlete's ability to overcome her physical limitations served as an *inspiration* to the children in the physical therapy group.
   - (A) humorous entertainment
   - (B) sense of hopelessness
   - (C) source of strong feelings or desires
   - (D) temporary change of daily activity

5. _____ **C** _____

6. The graduating seniors threw their caps wildly into the air and cheered loudly after every announcement. Meanwhile, on the stage, the speaker tried to maintain some *semblance* of order by reading his speech in a serious tone of voice.
   - (A) ability to withstand punishment
   - (B) outward appearance
   - (C) impossible assignment or mission
   - (D) loving and caring attitude

6. _____ **B** _____

7. The writer's work is full of tired, old *similes*. It does not take a genius to come up with the expressions "crazy like a fox" and "smooth as silk."
   - (A) comparisons using the words *like* or *as*
   - (B) punctuation marks
   - (C) animal characters that speak and act like humans
   - (D) simple rhymes and rhythms

7. _____ **A** _____

8. In order to *simulate* the feeling of weightlessness they would experience in space, the astronauts practiced performing their activities underwater.
   - (A) overcome through repeated efforts
   - (B) trick or deceive
   - (C) arouse
   - (D) imitate

8. _____ **D** _____

9. Because we had left for the evening, we knew nothing of what had *transpired* in our living room, but it appeared that our cats had had a fierce disagreement.
   - (A) put in rigid order
   - (B) occurred
   - (C) became transparent
   - (D) sought comfort and refreshment

9. _____ **B** _____

10. Some students find Shakespeare's plays difficult because the dialogue lacks *verisimilitude*. Real people do not go around saying "hark" and "forsooth."
    - (A) appearance of being genuine or real
    - (B) attractive appearance
    - (C) ruthless tactics
    - (D) religious value

10. _____ **A** _____

Applying Meaning

Follow the directions below to write a sentence using a vocabulary word.

1. Describe how you got an idea. Use any form of the word *inspiration*.
   Sample Answer: Seeing the look of satisfaction in my father's eyes as he finished the cabinet inspired me to be a carpenter.

2. Complete the sentence: One *simile* I often hear or read is "_____."
   Sample Answer: One simile I often hear or read is "It's as hard as a rock."

3. Write a sentence about a contest. Use any form of the word *aspirant*.
   Sample Answer: Hundreds of aspirants crowded into the room where the writing contest rules were to be announced.

4. Describe something that happened involving a license of some kind. Use any form of the word *expiration*.
   Sample Answer: Ed did not know his driver's license had expired until the police officer told him.

5. Write about something a coach might have players do to prepare for a game. Use any form of the word *simulate*.
   Sample Answer: Coach Sanchez made us run around the track carrying a sack of sand on our back to simulate the weight of the equipment we would wear in the game.

Read each sentence or short passage below. Write "correct" on the answer line if the vocabulary word has been used correctly. Write "incorrect" on the answer line if the vocabulary word has been used incorrectly.

6. When three schools closed, the fourth school had to *assimilate* several hundred students with different backgrounds and interests.

   6. ___correct___

7. The model airplane came with many parts to *ensemble*. It would take days to put it together.

   7. ___incorrect___

8. Many innings had *transpired* before our team even got a hit. It was little wonder that few spectators were around for the end of the game.

8. ___correct___

9. The painting did not have enough *verisimilitude* to be called realistic.

9. ___correct___

10. A *semblance* was held in the gym to commemorate Earth Day.

10. ___incorrect___

For each word used incorrectly, write a sentence using the word properly.

Answers will vary.

_____

_____

_____

_____

_____

_____

_____

Test-Taking Strategies

Some standardized tests ask you to choose the best word or words to complete a sentence. These tests are designed to check your ability to comprehend the slight differences in meaning among several words and their appropriateness for a particular context.

Sample

S. Able to sing, dance, and play piano, Fred Astaire was a _____ performer.
   (A) versatile   (B) popular
   (C) valuable   (D) demanding

S. _____A_____

Before answering, read the sentence carefully. Eliminate any answers that are clearly wrong. Then read the sentence to yourself, inserting your answer in the space to see if it is sensible and consistent with the entire sentence.

Practice: Choose the word or set of words that, when inserted in the sentence, *best* fits the meaning of the sentence as a whole.

1. Certain species of adult birds have been known to _____ an injury in order to lure predators away from their young.
   (A) inflict   (B) feign   (C) cause   (D) inspire

1. _____B_____

2. The sudden warming caused a _____ melting of the accumulated snow and brought about _____ flooding in certain areas.
   (A) rapid . . severe   (B) welcome . . mysterious
   (C) gradual . . expected   (D) necessary . . monotonous

2. _____A_____

3. The advertisement for home security alarms brazenly attempted to _____ homeowners into _____ an expensive burglar alarm.
   (A) inspire . . building   (B) provoke . . stealing
   (C) frighten . . purchasing (D) deceive . . operating

3. _____C_____

Name _____

How well do you remember the words you studied in Lessons 7 through 9?
Take the following test covering the words from the last three lessons.

Part 1 Choose the Correct Meaning

Each question below includes a word in capital letters, followed by four words
or phrases. Choose the word or phrase that is closest in meaning to the word
in capital letters. Write the letter for your answer on the line provided.

Sample

S. FINISH	(A) enjoy	(B) complete	**S.** ____B____
	(C) destroy	(D) enlarge	

1. SEMBLANCE	(A) musical group	(B) appearance	1. ____B____
	(C) familiar surroundings	(D) argument	
2. ASPIRANT	(A) someone seeking a goal	(B) type of medicine	2. ____A____
	(C) foolish person	(D) evil plot	
3. PROSECUTE	(A) pursue	(B) hurt repeatedly	3. ____C____
	(C) take legal action	(D) delay	
4. AUGUR	(A) drill	(B) forecast	4. ____B____
	(C) argue	(D) mythical beast	
5. FOUNDER	(A) stagger	(B) type of fish	5. ____C____
	(C) sink	(D) pioneer	
6. SIMULATE	(A) excite	(B) rearrange	6. ____D____
	(C) exaggerate	(D) imitate	
7. PRECEDE	(A) go before	(B) continue	7. ____A____
	(C) overcome	(D) anticipate	
8. INGENUOUS	(A) brilliant	(B) unsophisticated	8. ____B____
	(C) counterfeit	(D) easily injured	
9. BEVY	(A) shelter	(B) vigorous denial	9. ____C____
	(C) group	(D) bewitched	
10. PALATABLE	(A) portable	(B) agreeable to the taste	10. ____B____
	(C) suitable for a palace	(D) permissible	

Go on to next page. ➤

11. SIMILE (A) comparison (B) friendly gesture 11. ___**A**___
  (C) duplicate (D) simple

12. CUISINE (A) foreign diplomat (B) curiosity 12. ___**C**___
  (C) type of food (D) pleasing aroma

13. VERISIMILITUDE (A) high altitude (B) appearance of 13. ___**B**___
  being real

  (C) very similar (D) peculiar
  in appearance

14. GOSSAMER (A) device used in (B) type of bird 14. ___**D**___
  manufacturing

  (C) loud noises (D) light; filmy

15. AVERSE (A) having a strong (B) change direction 15. ___**A**___
  dislike

  (C) greedy (D) absent

Part 2 Matching Words and Meanings

Match the definition in Column B with the word in Column A.
Write the letter of the correct definition on the line provided.

Column A	**Column B**	
16. noxious	a. absorb; take in	**16.** ___e___
17. flounder	b. good idea or impulse	**17.** ___h___
18. persecute	c. come to pass; occur	**18.** ___d___
19. iridescent	d. mistreat	**19.** ___j___
20. careen	e. foul or harmful	**20.** ___g___
21. assimilate	f. clever	**21.** ___a___
22. transpire	g. lurch out of control	**22.** ___c___
23. proceed	h. move clumsily	**23.** ___i___
24. inspiration	i. continue; carry on	**24.** ___b___
25. ingenious	j. lustrous; rainbow-colored	**25.** ___f___

Name _____

Architecture in the Prairie Style

Among the arts, architecture is unique. Unlike the painter or the writer, the architect must first have a buyer and then satisfy the wishes of that client. In designing a building, the architect must **reconcile** his or her personal sense of art not only with the client's artistic sense, but with the
5   client's practical needs.

Perhaps because of this client-artist bond, architecture seems **inextricably** linked to the values and ideals of the culture that produced it. The ancient Greek emphasis on discipline and harmony is clearly visible in the balance and symmetry of the stately columns that have been **emulated** in so
10   many of our courthouses and government buildings.

Great architectural achievements have been historically associated with the huge and impressive structures in the midst of large, **densely** populated cities. However, Frank Lloyd Wright made his mark on the architectural world in the prairies of the Midwest. In fact, Wright **railed** against
15   the urban architectural environment.

As a young man, Wright traveled to Chicago in search of a position as an apprentice architect. In the late 1800s there could have been no better place for an **aspiring** architect. The great Chicago Fire of 1871 afforded architects the opportunity to rebuild a city, and they were doing it with
20   **unprecedented** creativity and ingenuity.

After spending some six years as a drafter, Wright set up his own practice in 1893. By 1910 he had achieved international recognition for his Prairie Style, which emphasized the harmonious relationship that must exist between a building's form and its function. This strong sense of the **intrinsic** rela-
25   tionship among form, function, and environment can be seen in all the houses he designed. A Frank Lloyd Wright house typically had a low, horizontal shape, which blended naturally with the open prairie. This sense of natural harmony also found **overt** expression in Wright's use of earth colors and wood.

30   Wright's most controversial structure is the Guggenheim Museum in New York City. This museum has been both criticized as a **grotesque** insult to the city and praised as one of the most remarkable feats of modern architecture. Whatever the judgment on Frank Lloyd Wright's work, he stands unequaled in his influence on modern architecture.

Words
aspire
dense
emulate
grotesque
inextricably
intrinsic
overt
rail
reconcile
unprecedented

Unlocking Meaning

Each word in this lesson's word list appears in dark type in the selection you just read. Think about how the vocabulary word is used in the selection, then write the letter for the best answer to each question.

1. In line 3, *reconcile* means _____.
   (A) argue vigorously   (B) compare
   (C) make consistent   (D) eliminate

   1. _____**C**_____

2. Which word could best replace *inextricably* in line 6?
   (A) inescapably   (B) invisibly
   (C) slightly   (D) foolishly

   2. _____**A**_____

3. Which word could best replace *emulated* in line 9?
   (A) ridiculed   (B) imitated
   (C) ignored   (D) reversed

   3. _____**B**_____

4. Which word could best replace *densely* in line 12?
   (A) thickly   (B) sparsely
   (C) happily   (D) beautifully

   4. _____**A**_____

5. Which word or words could best replace *railed* in line 14?
   (A) leaned   (B) contrasted
   (C) borrowed   (D) complained bitterly

   5. _____**D**_____

6. Which word could best replace *aspiring* in line 18?
   (A) ambitious   (B) untalented
   (C) aging   (D) unimaginative

   6. _____**A**_____

7. If something is *unprecedented* (line 20), it is _____.
   (A) unable to be understood   (B) unacceptable
   (C) without previous examples   (D) commonplace

   7. _____**C**_____

8. An *intrinsic* (line 24) relationship is one that is ____.
   (A) confusing   (B) essential
   (C) embarrassing   (D) amusing

   8. _____**B**_____

9. Which word could best replace *overt* in line 28?
   (A) open   (B) hidden
   (C) peculiar   (D) unappreciated

   9. _____**A**_____

10. Which word or words could best replace *grotesque* in line 31?
    (A) strange and ugly   (B) modern and stylish
    (C) historic   (D) sensational

    10. _____**A**_____

Name _____

Applying Meaning

Follow the directions below to write a sentence using a vocabulary word.

1. Describe a jungle or forest. Use any form of the word *dense*.

   Sample Answer: The dense growth of trees and bushes

   made walking through the forest very difficult.

2. Describe someone's goals or ambitions. Use any form of the word *aspire*.

   Sample Answer: It has always been Eduardo's aspiration

   to graduate from the United States Air Force Academy.

3. Describe a political speech about a proposed tax increase. Use any form of the word *rail*.

   Sample Answer: Senator Liu railed against the proposed

   tax increase, calling it an attempt to rob blue-collar

   workers.

4. Write a sentence giving some advice to a younger person about a role model. Use any form of the word *emulate*.

   Sample Answer: One should always be careful about

   choosing a role model to emulate.

Decide which word in parentheses best completes the sentence. Then write the sentence, adding the missing word.

5. Gloria's dislike for Enrique was ____ . She constantly criticized him in front of others and refused to be seen with him. (dense; overt)

   overt

6. The record-breaking snowfall last winter created an ____ demand for road salt. (inextricable; unprecedented)

   unprecedented

7. The clerk rechecked his calculations but still could not ____ the receipts with the money in the cash register. (emulate; reconcile)

reconcile
_____

_____

_____

8. Gold seems to have a certain ____ value. Throughout history it has been a symbol of wealth and power. (grotesque; intrinsic)

intrinsic
_____

_____

_____

9. The hostages posed an ____ problem for the president. Attacking the captors might harm the hostages; giving in to the demands would encourage the taking of more hostages. (inextricable; overt)

inextricable
_____

_____

_____

10. After the disastrous attack on the Confederate entrenchments at Fredericksburg, the battlefield was a(n) ____ combination of mangled corpses and desperate cries for help. (grotesque; intrinsic)

grotesque
_____

_____

_____

Mastering Meaning

In an encyclopedia or other source, find a picture of one of Frank Lloyd Wright's structures. It can be a house, an office building, or a public facility of some kind. Write a description of the structure, pointing out the elements that distinguish it from other structures. Note any elements that are part of Wright's Prairie Style.

Lesson

11

Part A

Name _____

In *Through the Looking-Glass,* one of Lewis Carroll's characters says, "Speak in French when you can't think of the English for a thing...." Over the centuries, speakers of English have done just that—borrowed words from French. This lesson focuses on ten words English has taken from French. In each case, no English word has quite the same meaning.

Unlocking Meaning

A vocabulary word appears in italics in each short passage below. Think about how the word is used in the passage. Then write a definition for the vocabulary word. Compare your definition with the definition on the flash card.

Words
au contraire
coup d'état
élan
esprit de corps
faux pas
laissez faire
nouveau riche
par excellence
savoir-faire
tête-à-tête

1. During the early part of the nineteenth century, the Democrats took a *laissez faire* approach to the economy and social issues. They felt that the problems of unemployment and poverty should be left to the natural laws of supply and demand. Creating new government programs would only delay the solution.

   Definitions will vary. _____

   _____

   _____

2. When a member of the committee began his response to the proposal by saying "*Au contraire,*" we knew we were about to hear another opinion. In fact, the two points of view on the problem were precisely opposite.

   Definitions will vary. _____

   _____

   _____

3. No one cooks better than my grandfather. His training in the great culinary schools of Paris have made him a chef *par excellence.*

   Definitions will vary. _____

   _____

   _____

4. Both gymnasts showed exceptional talent, but Jin's energy and style appealed to the judges. It was this *élan* that eventually won her the gold medal.

   Definitions will vary. _____

   _____

   _____

5. Ingrid always knows the right thing to say or do in awkward situations. Such *savoir-faire* will come in handy when she is interviewed by the scholarship committee.

Definitions will vary.

6. After the military staged a *coup d'état* and banished the elected president, the United States cut off all aid to the island country. Congress wanted to send a strong message of disapproval to those who had overthrown the government.

Definitions will vary.

7. Salvador and Dwayne talked privately for over two hours. None of us knew what they discussed in their *tête-à-tête*.

Definitions will vary.

8. Having trained and fought together for so long, the crew of the destroyer had developed a strong *esprit de corps*. Such loyalty and devotion allowed them to overcome difficulties that other crews would have been unable to handle.

Definitions will vary.

9. When Yori realized she was the only one wearing jeans at the party, she knew she had committed a *faux pas*. No one had told her that it was a formal affair.

Definitions will vary.

10. After winning the lottery, Jess bought an expensive new car and applied for membership at the exclusive country club. His application was turned down, however. The club's directors apparently disapprove of the *nouveau riche*. They prefer members who are accustomed to being wealthy.

Definitions will vary.

Applying Meaning

Decide which vocabulary word best completes each short passage below. Then write the last sentence in each passage, adding the missing word.

1. What a master of color and technique she is! No one else can paint like that! She is the best, truly an artist _____!

   par excellence _____

   _____

2. Our team has not played together very long. But with time and a lot of hard work we will develop the _____ needed to win games.

   esprit de corps _____

   _____

3. "But these are the facts! There is just one conclusion to be drawn," exclaimed Pedro.

   Alma just smiled and said, "_____, my friend—I see things a bit differently."

   Au contraire _____

   _____

4. Look at the huge tip that man wearing the expensive leather coat left me! I have never been fond of the _____, but I can certainly use the money.

   nouveau riche _____

   _____

5. The couple would never resolve their problems by screaming at each other in public. I suggested instead that they have a(n) _____ at home.

   tête-à-tête _____

   _____

6. The conspirators were so disorganized that they were soon captured by the president's security guards. Their feeble attempt at a(n) _____ failed before it ever got started.

   coup d'état _____

   _____

7. Cesar's parents decided not to interfere with his decision to let his hair grow. They were confident that their _____ approach would work when Cesar realized no one cared about his hair.

laissez faire _____

_____

8. The president appointed veteran legislator Amanda Rosen to the post of ambassador. He was sure her _____ would help overcome the prime minister's hostility.

savoir-faire _____

_____

9. First Adam tucked the napkin in the top of his shirt. Then he slurped his soup so loudly that everyone stared at him. He made one _____ after another.

faux pas _____

_____

10. The figure skaters demonstrated incredible energy and flair. It was certain that such _____ would not go unnoticed by the judges.

élan _____

_____

Our Living Language

noblesse oblige

The concepts of democracy and equality were almost unknown in the Middle Ages. Instead of authority rising from the consent of the people, it was thought to flow down from God through the king and the nobility. Being born to high rank, however, did carry with it a certain "obligation" to look after the commoners and peasants. This was not so much from a sense of goodwill or charity as it was from a feeling of superiority and "knowing what's best for them." This attitude became known by the French words *noblesse oblige,* meaning "nobility obligates."

Cooperative Learning: Do you think the attitude of *noblesse oblige* is alive today? Work with a partner to list some current examples of *noblesse oblige.* Do you sense it in certain government programs? Do certain school policies reflect this attitude?

Name _____

One of the more familiar Latin roots is *-flu-*, which comes from the Latin word *fluere,* meaning "to flow." This root also appears in English words as *-flux-* and *-fluct-*. Another Latin word, *flectere,* means "to bend" and usually appears as *-flect-* and *-flex-*. The vocabulary words in this lesson all have one of these roots.

Root	Meaning	English Word
-flu-	to flow	fluent
-flux-		influx
-fluct-		fluctuate
-flect-	to bend	genuflect
-flex-		reflex

Words
confluence
effluent
fluctuate
fluent
genuflect
inflexible
influx
mellifluous
reflex
superfluous

Unlocking Meaning

A vocabulary word appears in italics in each sentence or short passage below. Find the root in each vocabulary word and choose the letter for the correct definition. Write the letter for your choice on the answer line.

1. Thea gave several valid reasons about why she should be allowed to attend the concert. However, her parents remained *inflexible* about their decision, and Thea couldn't go.
   (A) silent
   (B) unwilling to change or bend
   (C) cooperative and helpful
   (D) willing to listen to reason

2. The temperature in April in New England often *fluctuates*. One day, the weather is warm; the next day the temperature drops below zero. Not even meteorologists seem able to predict what will happen.
   (A) rises and falls with no clear pattern
   (B) remains the same
   (C) defies established laws
   (D) imitates previous patterns

3. Felipe wrote a two-page response to the first test question. The first sentence gave all the information necessary to answer the question correctly. The rest of Felipe's lengthy response was *superfluous*.
   (A) necessary but incorrect
   (B) written out in longhand
   (C) well organized
   (D) more than is required

4. Between 1860 and 1890, there was an *influx* of immigrants into the United States. More than 10 million people from Ireland, England, Germany, and Scandinavia came to America during that time.
   (A) large-scale arrival or flowing in
   (B) exclusion or shutting out
   (C) widespread leaving
   (D) illegal prohibition

1. _____**B**_____

2. _____**A**_____

3. _____**D**_____

4. _____**A**_____

5. The map shows where Guggins Stream and Boxmill Stream come together. It is at this *confluence* that the town proposes to build a bridge.

    (A) impressive structure   (B) historic location

    (C) meeting place   (D) rise in the water level

5.   **C**

6. The girl scowled when the director called her onstage, and she looked anything but sweet. Everyone was shocked when she opened her mouth and a rich, *mellifluous* voice floated out.

    (A) cackling   (B) smooth and sweet

    (C) rough and irritating   (D) loud

6.   **B**

7. As was the custom, each visitor to the castle bowed before the king and knelt on one knee to show respect. The members of the court gasped in horror when the bold young woman refused to bow her head or *genuflect*.

    (A) depart on schedule   (B) stand straight and tall

    (C) speak insultingly   (D) touch a knee to the floor

7.   **D**

8. When the people in the town discovered that the river had been polluted by the *effluent* from factory pipes, they staged a protest and forced the company to find an environmentally safe way to dispose of its waste.

    (A) manufactured goods   (B) blockage

    (C) something that flows out   (D) excess material

8.   **C**

9. If a light is suddenly flashed in your face, the normal *reflex* is to blink. Another example of this kind of reaction is the sneeze.

    (A) difficulty   (B) automatic response

    (C) voluntary action   (D) willingness

9.   **B**

10. Debra speaks English, French, and Italian as if each of those were her first language. I wish I were *fluent* in more than one language.

    (A) able to speak with ease   (B) unable to speak easily

    (C) easily impressed   (D) talkative

10.   **A**

Name _____

Applying Meaning

Decide which word in parentheses best completes the sentence. Then write
the sentence, adding the missing word.

1. To become a good baseball player, you must overcome the normal
    _____ of ducking when the ball is hit toward you. (influx; reflex)

    reflex _____

    _____

    _____

2. The ceremony requires that worshipers _____ as they enter the
    shrine. (fluctuate; genuflect)

    genuflect _____

    _____

    _____

3. Keep your essay brief and do not include any _____ information.
    (mellifluous; superfluous)

    superfluous _____

    _____

    _____

4. I knew Tranh was stubborn, but I didn't think he would be so _____
    about changing his plans. (inflexible; mellifluous)

    inflexible _____

    _____

    _____

5. The Granite River has turned a murky brown as a result of the
    industrial _____ that flows into it. (effluent; fluent)

    effluent _____

    _____

    _____

6. During the summer, there is a great _____ of tourists to the tiny
    island. (influx; reflex)

    influx _____

    _____

    _____

Follow the directions below to write a sentence using a vocabulary word.

7. Describe an exchange student from a South American country. Use the word *fluent*.

   Sample Answer: Marco, the exchange student from Brazil, is fluent in Portuguese, Spanish, and English.

8. Use *fluctuate* in a sentence to describe the behavior of someone you know or might meet.

   Sample Answer: Kwam's moods fluctuate from extreme joy one minute to gloom and doom the next.

9. Describe something you feel is *mellifluous*.

   Sample Answer: The sound of Teresa's cello seemed especially mellifluous in last night's concert.

10. Write a sentence about fishing. Use the word *confluence*.

    Sample Answer: We pulled our canoe ashore at the confluence of the two rivers and fished there all afternoon.

Bonus Word

docudrama

Television has had a tremendous influence on language, adding many new words to our vocabulary. One word coined through television is *docudrama*. *Docudrama* is actually a combination of the word *documentary*, which comes from the Latin word *docere* meaning "to teach," and *drama* from the Greek root *-dran-* meaning "to perform." A docudrama is a dramatization of an event that actually happened.

Write a Paragraph: Think of an event in history that would make a good television docudrama. Write a paragraph explaining why you chose this event. Use some of the words you studied in this lesson.

10-12

How well do you remember the words you studied in Lessons 10 through 12? Take the following test covering the words from the last three lessons.

Part 1 Choose the Correct Meaning

Each question below includes a word in capital letters, followed by four words or phrases. Choose the word or phrase that is <u>closest</u> in meaning to the word in capital letters. Write the letter for your choice on the line provided.

Sample

S. FINISH	(A) enjoy	(B) complete	**S.**	**B**
	(C) destroy	(D) enlarge		

1. AU CONTRAIRE	(A) on the contrary	(B) I agree	**1.**	**A**
	(C) please leave	(D) good-bye		
2. INFLUX	(A) flexibility	(B) doubt	**2.**	**C**
	(C) flow	(D) insult		
3. RECONCILE	(A) understand	(B) make consistent	**3.**	**B**
	(C) exaggerate	(D) discover		
4. RAIL	(A) complain bitterly	(B) guide	**4.**	**A**
	(C) raid	(D) inform		
5. OVERT	(A) reversible	(B) completed	**5.**	**D**
	(C) bottomless	(D) obvious		
6. ÉLAN	(A) courage	(B) vigor	**6.**	**B**
	(C) inspiration	(D) awkward behavior		
7. GROTESQUE	(A) admirable	(B) enlarged	**7.**	**C**
	(C) strange and ugly	(D) highly prized		
8. COUP D' ÉTAT	(A) sudden overthrow of authority	(B) diplomatic mission	**8.**	**A**
	(C) container for important papers	(D) senseless violence		
9. GENUFLECT	(A) raise up	(B) verify as true	**9.**	**C**
	(C) touch one knee to the floor	(D) deflect		
10. EFFLUENT	(A) great wealth	(B) ability to speak well	**10.**	**D**
	(C) effective argument	(D) something that flows out		
11. ASPIRE	(A) to have ambition	(B) to dismiss casually	**11.**	**A**
	(C) to promote vigorously	(D) to die		

Go on to next page. ➤

12. LAISSEZ FAIRE   (A) laziness   (B) policy of noninterference   12. **B**

    (C) possessing great beauty   (D) ability to settle matters fairly

13. CONFLUENCE   (A) person with important influence   (B) convincing arguments   13. **C**

    (C) point where two streams flow together   (D) legal action against a government official

14. MELLIFLUOUS   (A) flowing sweetly and smoothly   (B) superstitious   14. **A**

    (C) easily melted   (D) able to speak many languages

15. INTRINSIC   (A) essential   (B) visible   15. **A**

    (C) hostile   (D) oddly shaped

Part 2 Matching Words and Meanings

Match the definition in Column B with the word in Column A.
Write the letter of the correct definition on the line provided.

Column A	Column B		
16. par excellence	a. automatic reaction	16.	d
17. superfluous	b. unnecessary	17.	b
18. inflexible	c. social skill	18.	g
19. faux pas	d. being the best of a kind	19.	e
20. emulate	e. minor blunder	20.	i
21. esprit de corps	f. having no previous example	21.	h
22. unprecedented	g. rigid	22.	f
23. reflex	h. common spirit of devotion	23.	a
24. savoir-faire	i. imitate	24.	c
25. fluctuate	j. vary irregularly	25.	j

Lesson
13
Part A

Name _____

The Spirit of 1215

The English barons who met at St. Albans outside London in 1213 cared little for the rights of the commoner. They only sought some **redress** from the excessive taxation, military service, and other demands King John was making on them. However, the articles they drafted in 1213 and were
5   approved by King John two years later eventually formed the foundation of our constitutional government. The revolutionary notions that all people are equal and that they possess certain **inviolable** rights beyond the power of ruler or church were born at this meeting.

The feudal society of thirteenth-century England demanded a baron's
10   loyalty to the king in return for land and a large share of the country's wealth. When King John came to power in 1199, however, he began making what the barons felt were excessive demands for military service and taxes. Perhaps an even more serious **provocation** was King John's refusal to consult his barons before altering accepted feudal laws and customs.

15   Such behavior might have been allowable in other circumstances, but English war losses to France had weakened the king's position and therefore **emboldened** the barons to draft 63 articles guaranteeing them certain rights. Once the articles were drafted, the barons **accosted** the king, demanding that he issue the articles as a royal charter to be distributed
20   throughout the kingdom. Under the **duress** of a faltering war abroad and civil strife at home, King John had little choice but to **acquiesce** to the barons' demands. So to **mollify** his nobility and keep his throne, King John approved the charter, known as the Magna Carta, in June 1215.

One article stated that the church should be free from royal interference.
25   Another stated that the king could not demand additional money from the barons without first consulting them. Yet another said that no one could be denied his property except by the lawful judgment of his equals. So in his effort to **obviate** a civil war, King John established democratic principles that the colonists carried to America several hundred years
30   later. In a very real sense, the spirit of 1776 got its start in 1215.

Only four original copies of the Magna Carta are **extant** today, all in England. Two are in the British Library, one is in Salisbury Cathedral, and one is in Lincoln Cathedral.

Words
accost
acquiesce
duress
embolden
extant
inviolable
mollify
obviate
provocation
redress

Unlocking Meaning

Each word in this lesson's word list appears in dark type in the selection you just read. Think about how the vocabulary word is used in the selection, then write the letter for the best answer to each question.

1. Which word or words could best replace *redress* in line 2?
   (A) punishment
   (B) increased interest
   (C) satisfaction for some wrong
   (D) amusement

   1. ____C____

2. An *inviolable* right (line 7) is one that _____ .
   (A) is rarely exercised
   (B) cannot be taken away
   (C) is not supported by law
   (D) is granted by the courts

   2. ____B____

3. Which words could best replace *provocation* in line 13?
   (A) source of anger
   (B) religious belief
   (C) idle thought
   (D) military action

   3. ____A____

4. Which word or words could best replace *emboldened* in line 17?
   (A) tricked
   (B) forced
   (C) strongly encouraged
   (D) frightened

   4. ____C____

5. If you *accost* an individual (line 18), you _____ .
   (A) confuse him or her
   (B) punish him or her severely
   (C) entertain him or her
   (D) approach him or her angrily

   5. ____D____

6. Which word or words could best replace *duress* in line 20?
   (A) supervision
   (B) threat
   (C) pleasant surroundings
   (D) sense of duty

   6. ____B____

7. If you *acquiesce* (line 21) to something, you _____ .
   (A) ignore it completely
   (B) boast about it
   (C) gaze at it lovingly
   (D) quietly agree to it

   7. ____D____

8. Which word or words could best replace *mollify* in line 22?
   (A) soothe or comfort
   (B) make angry
   (C) insult
   (D) confuse or bewilder

   8. ____A____

9. If you *obviate* a risk (line 28), you _____ .
   (A) increase it
   (B) prevent it
   (C) defeat it
   (D) embrace it

   9. ____B____

10. If something is *extant* (line 31), it is _____ .
    (A) misplaced
    (B) illegible
    (C) still in existence
    (D) worshiped

    10. ____C____

Applying Meaning

Read each sentence or short passage below. Write "correct" on the answer line if the vocabulary word has been used correctly. Write "incorrect" on the answer line if the vocabulary word has been used incorrectly.

1. After the thunderstorm passed, the kindergarten teacher tried to *mollify* the frightened children by playing the piano and singing a happy song.

2. One theory suggests that a meteor struck the earth and the resulting smoke caused the dinosaur to become *extant*.

3. The disgruntled worker *accosted* the supervisor at the factory gate and attempted to engage him in a fight, but the supervisor simply walked away and fired the worker the following morning.

4. The students felt a great sense of *duress* when they learned everyone had passed the test.

5. The owner insisted that Brutus was a kind and gentle dog who would never attack someone without some *provocation*.

6. The dwindling number of police officers patrolling the streets only *emboldened* the thieves. Now stores were being robbed in broad daylight.

7. In order to *obviate* the "no hunting" signs on his property, the farmer painted them a brilliant orange and placed them around his farm at ten-foot intervals.

8. Before the mayor would *acquiesce* to the city council's plan, she insisted that the citizens have an opportunity to voice their opinions in a town meeting.

9. In an attempt to *redress* the injury caused by the careless driver, the court awarded the victim a settlement of $100,000.

10. The ring was not worth a great deal of money to someone else, but its sentimental value to the family made it *inviolable*.

1. __correct__

2. __incorrect__

3. __correct__

4. __incorrect__

5. __correct__

6. __correct__

7. __incorrect__

8. __correct__

9. __correct__

10. __incorrect__

For each word used incorrectly, write a sentence using the word properly.
Answers will vary.

_____

_____

_____

_____

_____

_____

_____

_____

_____

_____
_____
_____
_____
_____
_____

Each question below contains at least one vocabulary word from this lesson. Answer each question "yes" or "no" in the space provided.

11. If someone with a club *accosted* you, would you be under some *duress?*

11. ___**yes**___

12. If someone destroyed the only *extant* copy of George Washington's diary, could the owner seek *redress?*

12. ___**yes**___

13. After hundreds of years will dead trees and animals turn hard and *mollify?*

13. ___**no**___

14. Does the Declaration of Independence indicate that life, liberty, and the pursuit of happiness are *inviolable* rights?

14. ___**yes**___

For each question you answered "no," write a sentence using the vocabulary word(s) correctly.

Answers will vary.

_____
_____
_____
_____
_____

Mastering Meaning

Look up some information on feudal laws and customs. Then compare feudal society to our own democratic society. Draw a line down the middle of a page. Label one column "feudal society" and the other "democratic society" and list as many points of comparison as possible. For example, in the feudal world, the king held all authority. In a democracy, authority lies with the individual and is expressed through a vote. When you have finished, use your notes to write an essay using some of the words you studied in this lesson.

Name _____

Human experience consists largely of finding, making, and remaking connections among ideas, observations, and objects. The variety and number of those connections are seemingly endless. In this lesson you will study ten words, each of which stands for one of the many ways to combine and connect the things around us.

Unlocking Meaning

Read the sentences or short passages below. Write the letter for the correct definition of the italicized vocabulary word.

You see it on television, billboards, buses, magazines, and blimps. Advertising is so *pervasive* in our society it would be a mistake to underestimate its influence.

1. (A) offensive to good taste
   (B) thoroughly present
   (C) rare and unusual
   (D) often misunderstood

The ability to get and keep a good job seems to *correlate* with the education one has received. This is just one more reason to stay in school.

2. (A) compete
   (B) eliminate; do away
   (C) have a relationship
   (D) have a corrupting influence

Thanks to the strong tide and surface winds, the oil spill was quickly *diffused* over a larger area of the ocean. Had the oil slick blown ashore, much wildlife would have been destroyed.

3. (A) spread out
   (B) reported
   (C) confined to specified limits
   (D) mistakenly observed

To our surprise, the orange juice we bought had been *adulterated* with water and sugar. In addition to tasting bad, the juice lacked vitamins and other nutrients.

4. (A) improved substantially by combining with other substances
   (B) spoiled through lack of refrigeration
   (C) mislabeled or confused
   (D) made impure by low-quality ingredients

Words

adulterate
amalgamate
coalesce
correlate
diffuse
disseminate
ligature
periphery
permeate
pervasive

1. ___B___

2. ___C___

3. ___A___

4. ___D___

In order to protect the park from the noise and pollution that accompany large numbers of automobiles, visitors were required to park their cars in one of the lots located on the park's *periphery* and hike to the interior.

5. (A) center
   (B) surrounding area
   (C) carefully landscaped environment
   (D) recreational and picnic area

5. _____ **B** _____

Three marching bands, four floats, and a fire truck will *coalesce* to form the Fourth of July parade.

6. (A) come together; unite
   (B) scatter
   (C) disappear
   (D) face one another

6. _____ **A** _____

The two small school districts decided to *amalgamate*. It was more efficient to operate a single, large school system than two smaller systems.

7. (A) compete in an open market
   (B) disintegrate entirely
   (C) mix or combine
   (D) subdivide into smaller units

7. _____ **C** _____

Finding a treatment for the new strain of flu was not enough. Information about the treatment had to be *disseminated* to doctors throughout the world before another outbreak occurred.

8. (A) denied
   (B) sold
   (C) spread
   (D) translated

8. _____ **C** _____

Before the recycling truck would pick up our old newspapers, we had to secure them with a *ligature* to make them easier to handle and to keep them from blowing all over the neighborhood.

9. (A) strong or forceful lecture
   (B) illegal substance
   (C) quiet or comforting remark
   (D) something used to tie or bind

9. _____ **D** _____

After the game, a mood of gloom and frustration *permeated* the locker room. All of the team members wondered quietly how they could have blown a 20-point halftime lead and lost the most important game of the year.

10. (A) disappeared from
    (B) spread throughout
    (C) avoided
    (D) enthusiastically embraced

10. _____ **B** _____

Applying Meaning

Follow the directions below to write a sentence using a vocabulary word.

1. Describe the role a newspaper might play in an emergency. Use any form of the word *disseminate*.

Sample Answer: After the snowstorm, the *Middletown Bugle* played an important role in disseminating information about the school closings.

2. Use the word *periphery* to describe one feature of an imaginary garden.

Sample Answer: A white picket fence was installed around the periphery of the garden to keep rabbits out.

3. Write a sentence about the role of some type of diet in maintaining good health. Use any form of the word *correlate*.

Sample Answer: It is best to eat low-fat foods because there is a high correlation between fat in the diet and heart attacks.

4. Tell about the influence of some well-known person or event on people. Use any form of the word *pervasive*.

Sample Answer: The effects of the stock market crash of 1929 pervaded every aspect of American society for many years.

5. Describe one way to reorganize the classes in a school. Use any form of the word *amalgamate*.

Sample Answer: The first- and second-grade classes were amalgamated into a single grade.

6. Describe how to package something. Use the word *ligature*.

Sample Answer: To be sure the suitcase would not fall off the luggage rack, we tightened the ligature one more time.

Each question below contains a vocabulary word from this lesson. Answer each question "yes" or "no" in the space provided.

7. Would a dictator want rebellious citizens to *coalesce* into an army?

7. ____**no**____

8. If someone cooked several cloves of garlic, would the smell of garlic *permeate* the house?

8. ____**yes**____

9. Is it possible for a child to *adulterate* a beverage?

9. ____**yes**____

10. Is the town square usually located on the *periphery* of a town?

10. ____**no**____

11. Could a strong wind *diffuse* a group of sailboats attempting to cross a large body of water?

11. ____**yes**____

12. Must you have a driver's license before you can *correlate*?

12. ____**no**____

For each question you answered "no," write a sentence using the vocabulary word correctly.

Answers will vary.

_____

_____

_____

_____

_____

_____

_____

_____

_____

Bonus Words

aboveboard   **undermine**

Gamblers first used the term *aboveboard* to refer to the placement of the players' hands in a card game. When the hands were aboveboard and in plain view, they could not engage in some trick such as pulling cards from a sleeve. Now the term refers to any straightforward or honest manner.

The word *undermine* was first used in warfare to describe a secret tunnel dug beneath the walls of a fort or castle in order to weaken or collapse it. Now it refers to weakening or harming something by some secret process.

Write a Paragraph: Describe how something was undermined or give an example of how something can be kept aboveboard.

Name _____

The Greek root *-ec-*, which appears at the beginning of several familiar words, comes from the Greek word *ektos,* meaning "out." Words for surgical procedures that "take out" something also contain this root. Another Greek root that you often see at the beginning of words is *-eu-,* which means "good." The vocabulary words in this lesson all have one of these roots.

Root	Meaning	English Word
-ec-	out	ecstatic
		appendectomy
-eu-	good, well	euphoria

Unlocking Meaning

Write the vocabulary word that fits each clue below. Then say the word and write a short definition. Compare your definition and pronunciation with those given on the flash card.

1. This adjective is a combination of two Greek elements. One is the Greek word *legein,* which means "to gather" or "to collect." The other is the *-ec-* root. A literal translation of this word would be "select out."

   eclectic. Definitions will vary.
   _____
   _____

2. The Greek word *euphoros,* meaning "healthy," can be seen in this word. It is reasonable to assume that a healthy person would feel "good."

   euphoria. Definitions will vary.
   _____
   _____

3. The noun form of this word is "ecstasy." Synonyms include "enraptured" and "blissful."

   ecstatic. Definitions will vary.
   _____
   _____

4. This noun names a surgical procedure. It contains the Greek root for "out" and the Latin word *appendere,* from which we get the word *appendix,* an organ in the body.

   appendectomy. Definitions will vary.
   _____
   _____

Words

appendectomy

eccentric

eclectic

eclipse

ecstatic

eulogize

euphemism

euphoria

euthanasia

mastectomy

5. This word, which can be a verb or a noun, came into the English language from the Greek word *ekleipein*, meaning "to fail to appear."

   eclipse. Definitions will vary.

   _____

   _____

6. This word also names a surgical procedure. The word begins with the Greek word *mastos*, meaning "breast."

   mastectomy. Definitions will vary.

   _____

   _____

7. This word contains a form of the Greek word *thanatos*, which means "death." It literally means "good death" because some people believe death is better than suffering with an incurable disease.

   euthanasia. Definitions will vary.

   _____

   _____

8. This verb came into English through the Greek word *eulogia*, meaning "praise." It is usually associated with praise afforded someone who has died.

   eulogize. Definitions will vary.

   _____

   _____

9. This adjective comes from a combination of the Greek root -*ec*- and the Greek word *kentrom*, meaning "center," so it implies that something is out of balance or off-center. It is often used to describe the behavior of some millionaires who prefer to appear impoverished.

   eccentric. Definitions will vary.

   _____

   _____

10. This word's Greek roots literally translate as "good speech." An example of one is saying a loved one has "passed on" when in reality she has died.

    euphemism. Definitions will vary.

    _____

    _____

Name _____

Applying Meaning

Read each sentence or short passage below. Write "correct" on the answer line if the vocabulary word has been used correctly. Write "incorrect" on the answer line if the vocabulary word has been used incorrectly.

1. The surgeon explained to Ms. Asari that the results of her breast biopsy were negative. She would not need a *mastectomy*.

   1. _____**correct**_____

2. Just as predicted, there was a total *eulogy* of the moon on Thursday night.

   2. ___**incorrect**___

3. Hester seemed embarrassed to tell people that she was a funeral director. She preferred the *euphemism* "final arrangements counselor."

   3. _____**correct**_____

4. The doctor insisted that it was her job to save and extend lives. She would never engage in *euthanasia*.

   4. _____**correct**_____

5. The television picture was *ecstatic* whenever a plane flew over the house. It was impossible to watch TV at such times.

   5. ___**incorrect**___

6. As he grew older, the scientist grew more and more *eccentric*. He let his hair grow down to his waist and ate nothing but rice and fish.

   6. _____**correct**_____

7. The old castle was decorated in an *eclectic* style, with pieces of furniture representing every major period in European history.

   7. _____**correct**_____

8. If you are not sure of the answer, go to the library and look up the topic in an *appendectomy*.

   8. ___**incorrect**___

9. The man was in a state of *euphoria*. Who wouldn't be after winning $30 million?

   9. _____**correct**_____

10. The *eclipse* started at 10:30 at night. By 1:00 A.M., the moon was totally obscured by the shadow of the earth.

   10. _____**correct**_____

For each word used incorrectly, write a sentence using the word properly.

Answers will vary.

_____

_____

_____

_____

_____

_____

_____

_____

_____

_____

_____

_____

_____

_____

_____

Decide which word in parentheses best completes the   sentence. Then
write the sentence, adding the missing word.

11. The critic claimed to have _____ tastes in music. Some rock groups, he
felt, were as talented as classical artists. (eclectic; ecstatic)

eclectic_____

_____

_____

12. The president himself offered to deliver the _____ at the war hero's
funeral. (eulogy; euphemism)

eulogy_____

_____

_____

Our Living Language

Euphemisms are usually an honest attempt to avoid hurting someone's
feelings with a harsh word. Sometimes, however, euphemisms can mislead or attempt to conceal the true meaning of something. For example,
a senator may claim he supports "revenue enhancements" instead of
saying he favors new taxes. See if you can figure out what these
euphemisms really mean:

involuntary, permanent downsizing	**firing employees**
total, permanent incapacitation	**death**
reality augmentation	**lying**
ethnic cleansing	**killing members of an ethnic group**
nuclear device	**bomb**

13-15

How well do you remember the words you studied in Lessons 13 through 15? Take the following test covering the words from the last three lessons.

Part 1 Choose the Correct Meaning

Each question below includes a word in capital letters, followed by four words or phrases. Choose the word or phrase that is <u>closest</u> in meaning to the word in capital letters. Write the letter for your answer on the line provided.

Sample

S. FINISH	(A) enjoy	(B) complete	S.	**B**
	(C) destroy	(D) send		

1. EUPHEMISM	(A) merciful death	(B) kind or gentle word	1.	**B**
	(C) loud argument	(D) religious belief		
2. ADULTERATE	(A) grow older	(B) add inferior ingredients to something	2.	**B**
	(C) misbehave	(D) purify by applying heat		
3. EULOGIZE	(A) praise highly	(B) simplify and improve	3.	**A**
	(C) energize	(D) hypnotize		
4. DURESS	(A) doubt	(B) threat	4.	**B**
	(C) intelligence	(D) convincing arguments		
5. ECCENTRIC	(A) conspicuous	(B) stressed or accented	5.	**D**
	(C) ordinary	(D) strange or unusual		
6. PERIPHERY	(A) outer region	(B) pleasant outlook	6.	**A**
	(C) patience	(D) exact information		
7. ACCOST	(A) charge illegally high fees	(B) approach angrily	7.	**B**
	(C) rearrange	(D) refuse to recognize		
8. EUPHORIA	(A) harmonious musical sounds	(B) unnecessary words	8.	**C**
	(C) feeling of well-being	(D) harmless curiosity		
9. MOLLIFY	(A) to insult	(B) to calm and comfort	9.	**B**
	(C) to decide quickly	(D) to betray		

Go on to next page. ➤

10. PERVASIVE   (A) frequently imitated   (B) present throughout   10. _____**B**_____
                    (C) easily persuaded   (D) misleading

11. LIGATURE   (A) person involved in   (B) part of the leg   11. _____**D**_____
                      legal action
                    (C) written message   (D) item used to tie
                                               or bind

12. ACQUIESCE   (A) to intermingle   (B) to come to know   12. _____**C**_____
                      (C) to agree to   (D) to submit for
                                               approval

13. AMALGAMATE   (A) intermix   (B) comfort   13. _____**A**_____
                      (C) agree to compromise (D) insist

14. APPENDECTOMY   (A) lengthy speech   (B) part of a book   14. _____**D**_____
                      (C) serious criminal   (D) surgical removal
                           action   of the appendix

15. EXTANT   (A) in existence   (B) extinct   15. _____**A**_____
                      (C) old-fashioned   (D) placed out of sight

Part 2 Matching Words and Meanings

Match the definition in Column B with the word in Column A.
Write the letter of the correct answer on the line provided.

Column A	Column B	
16. correlate	a. source of irritation or anger	16. _____h_____
17. redress	b. to spread throughout	17. _____d_____
18. obviate	c. mercy killing	18. _____g_____
19. eclectic	d. remedy for a wrong	19. _____j_____
20. euthanasia	e. to block out or cover	20. _____c_____
21. ecstatic	f. untouchable	21. _____i_____
22. provocation	g. prevent	22. _____a_____
23. diffuse	h. to relate one thing to another	23. _____b_____
24. eclipse	i. overjoyed	24. _____e_____
25. inviolable	j. taken from several sources	25. _____f_____

Name _____

Too Many Deer

The deer were beautiful, with big, soft eyes and **tawny** brown coats. Every evening they emerged from the forest preserve to feed on the **succulent** plants in the yards of neighboring homes. In the spring, each doe was faithfully followed by a pair of young. Protected by the camouflage of their
5   coat and total lack of scent, they were rarely detected by most predators.

For a few years this picturesque scene persisted as deer **gamboled** playfully among suburban yards, to the delight of fascinated onlookers. Every year the audience observed more and more deer. With the increased population, the search for food intensified. Soon the deer began treating the trees
10 and plants as a kind of **commissary** offering a variety of foods. In addition, the deer did not frolic playfully anymore. Their eyes were not clear, and their coats were scraggly. What had happened and why?

If left unchecked, any living population multiplies until it meets or exceeds the ability of the environment to support it. This is especially true when
15 all natural enemies have been eliminated. People, in general, have been good to the deer, **excising** the thick undergrowth from forests and eliminating predators such as the wolf. Deer thrive under these conditions and soon reach a state of overpopulation. However, with **rigorous** management, the excess population can be controlled by harvesting a specified
20 number of deer or by introducing predators.

But this is not just a story about deer. Human beings are subject to the same rules as every other living population. More than 150 years ago Thomas Malthus, a British scholar, was alarmed by what he saw happening to human populations. To his **consternation**, his projections indicated that human
25 populations would soon exceed the food supply, which could result in war, disease, and starvation. Fortunately, Malthus's projections did not come to pass because technology has allowed us to produce food more efficiently than he projected. However, he may not have been wrong — just ahead of his time. Recently, Worldwatch, an environmental organization,
30 released a study that showed we may be approaching the limit of what technology can do to increase the food supply. Despite high-yield grains, the per capita amount of rice and wheat are falling, and we are already taking about as many fish from the sea as we should if we wish to avoid damaging the breeding stock. In addition, as farmland is destroyed by ero-
35 sion and industrialization, the earth is losing its **agrarian** potential.

To **ameliorate** this problem, we must begin to produce food as efficiently as possible and to avoid waste. If we are not **prudent** about our choices, nature will take steps to adjust the imbalance.

Words
agrarian
ameliorate
commissary
consternation
excise
gambol
prudent
rigorous
succulent
tawny

Each word in this lesson's word list appears in dark type in the selection you just read. Think about how the vocabulary word is used in the selection, then write the letter for the best answer to each question.

1. Which word could best replace *tawny* in line 1?
   (A) ugly   (B) invisible
   (C) golden   (D) happy

   1. _____ **C** _____

2. Which word could best replace *succulent* in line 2?
   (A) inedible   (B) thorny
   (C) poisonous   (D) juicy

   2. _____ **D** _____

3. Which word could best replace *gamboled* in line 6?
   (A) frolicked   (B) collapsed
   (C) argued   (D) hid

   3. _____ **A** _____

4. Which word or words could best replace *commissary* in line 10?
   (A) nursery   (B) meeting room
   (C) source of food (D) burial ground

   4. _____ **C** _____

5. Which word or words could best replace *excising* in line 16?
   (A) adding   (B) exercising
   (C) organizing   (D) cutting out

   5. _____ **D** _____

6. In line 18, the word *rigorous* means _____ .
   (A) expensive   (B) strict
   (C) disorganized   (D) sloppy

   6. _____ **B** _____

7. In line 24, the word *consternation* means _____ .
   (A) relief   (B) alarm
   (C) amusement   (D) excitement

   7. _____ **B** _____

8. Which word or words could best replace *agrarian* in line 35?
   (A) agricultural   (B) possibility for happiness
   (C) criminal   (D) architectural

   8. _____ **A** _____

9. Which word could best replace *ameliorate* in line 36?
   (A) disguise   (B) relieve
   (C) exaggerate   (D) highlight

   9. _____ **B** _____

10. In line 37, the word *prudent* means _____ .
   (A) wasteful   (B) wise
   (C) reckless   (D) careless

   10. _____ **B** _____

Name _____

Applying Meaning

Follow the directions below to write a sentence using a vocabulary word.

1. Tell about the aftermath of a disaster. Use any form of the word *ameliorate* in your answer.

   Sample Answer: The Red Cross shelter ameliorated the

   housing shortage after the earthquake.

   _____

2. Use the word *commissary* in a sentence about a place you visit or pass regularly.

   Sample Answer: Our school cafeteria is not my favorite

   commissary.

   _____

3. Tell about waiting in a long line. Use any form of the word *consternation* in your answer.

   Sample Answer: Our consternation grew when we found

   that the line at the theater stretched around the block.

   _____

4. Describe an important change you have made in your life. Use any form of the word *excise*.

   Sample Answer: I began to lose weight when I excised

   candy from my diet.

   _____

5. Describe children playing in the park. Use any form of the word *gambol*.

   Sample Answer: Dozens of happy children gamboled

   noisily in the park playground.

   _____

6. Tell about a dangerous situation you or someone else avoided. Use the word *prudent* in your answer.

   Sample Answer: When the waves rose to three feet, we

   decided that the prudent thing to do was to return to

   the harbor.

---

7. Describe a beautiful animal. Use the word *tawny* in your sentence.

Sample Answer: The lion at the zoo has a sleek, tawny coat.

Read each sentence below. Write "correct" on the answer line if the vocabulary word has been used correctly. Write "incorrect" on the answer line if the vocabulary word has been used incorrectly.

8. The new president promised *agrarian* reforms that would give land to anyone who promised to farm it.

8. _____correct_____

9. A balanced diet and *excise* are good ways to build a healthy body.

9. _____incorrect_____

10. After the enemy began to fire on their position, the soldiers were forced to *gambol* into their trenches.

10. _____incorrect_____

11. Taking a *rigorous* course in mathematics is excellent preparation for the difficult courses one encounters in college.

11. _____correct_____

12. Dan's favorite part of a peach is the *succulent* center near the seed.

12. _____correct_____

For each word used incorrectly, write a sentence using the word properly.

Answers will vary.

Mastering Meaning

In some forest preserves and other areas, the deer population has grown so great that many deer face starvation. One proposed solution to this overpopulation problem is to allow occasional hunting in these areas. What do you think of this solution? Can you think of a better one? Write a short essay explaining your position on this issue. Use some of the words you studied in this lesson.

Name _____

Criticism comes in many varieties. Some criticism is purposeful and helpful, while some is offensive and resented. The English language is full of words to describe how people criticize others and the types of criticism they offer. In this lesson you will learn ten words having to do with criticism.

Unlocking Meaning

Read the sentences or short passages below. Write the letter for the correct definition of the italicized vocabulary word.

Although his heartbroken father *remonstrated* with Vladimir for hours, the boy held fast to his decision. In spite of his father's arguments, he was going to join the army rather than go to college.

1. (A) praised and complimented a course of action
   (B) supported financially
   (C) presented strong reasons in objection to something
   (D) failed to carry out a promise or obligation

The judge would not allow cameras at the trial. She felt that they would distract the jury and *impeach* the integrity of the court itself.

2. (A) enhance
   (B) bring discredit upon
   (C) ignore and embarrass
   (D) publicize

The dispute over Grandmother's will grew *acrimonious* when Leo accused Luis of taking advantage of Grandmother when she was ill. Leo even said that Luis convinced Grandmother to invest in Luis's failing business.

3. (A) bitter, sharp
   (B) marked by moderation and restraint
   (C) sentimental
   (D) humorous

"Look at this article!" the actor yelled, waving the tabloid in the air. "It says that I was fired from a movie for being nasty and uncooperative. Why, that's totally false! I should sue this paper for *defaming* my character!"

4. (A) praising faintly or halfheartedly
   (B) saying the opposite of what is really intended
   (C) expressing remorse or contrition
   (D) attacking the good name of someone by slander or libel

Words
acrimonious
aspersion
censure
critique
defame
deride
impeach
innuendo
remonstrate
upbraid

1. _____C_____

2. _____B_____

3. _____A_____

4. _____D_____

The other members of the school board could no longer tolerate the slanderous remarks of the chairperson. A formal resolution that was introduced to *censure* his behavior passed overwhelmingly.

5. (A) praise publicly

   (B) officially disapprove of

   (C) recognize through an award

   (D) imitate

5. _____**B**_____

After the first performance of the play, the cast waited anxiously to read the *critiques* in the press. If they were favorable, the play would have a long run. If they were not, the cast could begin packing.

6. (A) critical reviews or comments

   (B) advertisements

   (C) explanations of confusing events

   (D) formal apologies

6. _____**A**_____

The mother was so relieved to recover her lost child that she found it difficult to *upbraid* the youngster for running off, even though she knew he clearly deserved it.

7. (A) scold

   (B) congratulate

   (C) speak words of comfort

   (D) turn away from

7. _____**A**_____

Amit's career as a medical researcher was almost ruined when a jealous colleague cast *aspersions* about the honesty of Amit's methods and results. However, an investigation showed that Amit's work was faultless.

8. (A) compliments

   (B) comparisons to accepted experts

   (C) weak threats

   (D) injurious or damaging remarks

8. _____**D**_____

The day before the election, Senator Barker's opponent asked how the senator could afford a new home and fancy automobile on a state senator's salary. Senator Barker deeply resented such an *innuendo*, claiming he earned the money honestly.

9. (A) profitable activity

   (B) bombastic oratory or rhetoric

   (C) indirect, often damaging suggestion

   (D) silly remark

9. _____**C**_____

Yan *derided* the training he had received at the survival camp. He made fun of the songs and ceremonies and claimed that most campers ate at the nearby hamburger stand.

10. (A) spoke in defense of

   (B) showed disdain through ridicule and humor

   (C) recommended strongly

   (D) pretended to enjoy

10. _____**B**_____

Applying Meaning

Read each sentence below. Write "correct" on the answer line if the vocabulary word has been used correctly. Write "incorrect" on the answer line if the vocabulary word has been used incorrectly.

1. The party deteriorated into an *acrimonious* debate over curfews.

2. At the soldier's funeral, his friends *upbraided* him for his courage.

3. Several students *remonstrated* their support for the teacher by writing letters of praise to the school board.

4. The applicant had an *unimpeachable* record with his previous employer, so I recommended we hire him.

5. The lawyer was quite unhappy about the *aspersions* the newspaper made about her client before the trial even began.

6. A good public relations agency will be sure that newspaper articles and television reports *defame* its clients on a regular basis.

7. At her going-away party, the woman's many friends *derided* her as someone they could always turn to in time of need.

8. After hearing one *innuendo* after another, the politician demanded that the prosecutor either charge him with a crime or keep quiet.

9. As part of the final exam, we had to write a *critique* of *Macbeth*.

10. The profanity should be *censured* before the book is assigned.

1.   **correct**

2.   **incorrect**

3.   **incorrect**

4.   **correct**

5.   **correct**

6.   **incorrect**

7.   **incorrect**

8.   **correct**

9.   **correct**

10.   **incorrect**

For each word used incorrectly, write a sentence using the word properly.

Answers will vary.

_____

_____

_____

_____

_____

_____

_____

_____

_____

_____

_____

_____

_____

_____

_____

Write each sentence below. In the space write a form of the word in parentheses. The form of the word in parentheses may be correct.

11. In all my years in politics, I have never witnessed such ___ in a debate. (acrimonious)

    In all my years in politics, I had never witnessed such

    acrimony in a debate.

12. The president of the company sued the newspaper for the _____ of his reputation. (defame)

    The president of the company sued the newspaper for

    the defamation of his reputation.

13. The mayor thought appointing his brother to the commission could _____ the integrity of his entire administration. (impeach)

    The mayor thought appointing his brother to the

    commission could impeach the integrity of his entire

    administration.

14. Jasper could hear the _____ in his mother's voice as the conversation turned to his report card. (deride)

    Jasper could hear the derision in his mother's voice as

    the conversation turned to his report card.

⬤	***Bonus Word***
	muckraker
	A character with a muck-rake in John Bunyan's *The Pilgrim's Progress* is so
	busy raking the muck and filth of the world that he is unable to raise his
	eyes to heaven. When certain American writers in the early 1900s ex-
	posed unsafe working conditions and political corruption, President
	Theodore Roosevelt denounced these journalists as *muckrakers*
	concerned only with finding "filth." Some politicians today still refer to
	anyone exposing corruption and social ills as a muckraker.
	Cooperative Learning: Draft a letter to your local or school paper expos-
	ing some situation you feel needs to be changed. Share your draft with a
	partner and critique each other's drafts. Then revise your letter as your
	partner suggests.

Name _____

Mark Antony begins his famous speech in *Julius Caesar* with the words "Friends, Romans, countrymen, lend me your ears." The citizens of Rome loved a good speech, even on an unhappy occasion such as the death of Caesar. Many of our English words about speech and speaking come from two Latin words: the word *loqui,* meaning "to speak," and the word *dicere,* meaning "to say." The vocabulary words in this lesson come from one of these two words.

Root	Meaning	English Word
-loqu- -locu-	to speak	loquacious elocution
-dict-	to say	dictum

Unlocking Meaning

Write the vocabulary word that fits each clue below. Then say the word and write a short definition. Compare your definition and pronunciation with those given on the flash card.

1. This noun begins with the Latin root *-mal-,* meaning "bad," so a literal translation of its roots would be "bad say."

   malediction. Definitions will vary. _____

   _____

   _____

2. Someone with authority must issue this kind of announcement, which combines the prefix *e-,* meaning "out," with the root meaning "to say."

   edict. Definitions will vary. _____

   _____

   _____

3. A person with this quality can talk around a topic without really addressing it. You see the same root in this word as you see in the word "circle."

   circumlocution. Definitions will vary. _____

   _____

   _____

4. This adjective might be used to describe someone whom you would like to be quiet.

   loquacious. Definitions will vary. _____

   _____

   _____

Words

circumlocution

colloquium

contradict

dictate

dictum

edict

elocution

interdict

loquacious

malediction

5. This noun comes to us unchanged from the past participle of the Latin verb *dicere*. An example of one is "If it sounds too good to be true, it probably is."

dictum. Definitions will vary.

_____

_____

6. This noun is usually associated with an academic or scholarly group. The *col-* prefix, meaning "with" or "together," makes the word translate literally as "speaking together."

colloquium. Definitions will vary.

_____

_____

7. This word comes to us from the Latin through the Old French word *entredit*, meaning "to forbid." Today this verb is usually used by legal authorities.

interdict. Definitions will vary.

_____

_____

8. This noun also has the *e-* prefix you see in "edict." In fact, a mastery of this art would be very helpful to a person who has to deliver edicts.

elocution. Definitions will vary.

_____

_____

9. This word, related to *dictum*, can be a noun or a verb.

dictate. Definitions will vary.

_____

_____

10. This word is formed by adding the Latin prefix *contra-*, meaning "against," to the root meaning "to say."

contradict. Definitions will vary.

_____

_____

Applying Meaning

Follow the directions below to write a sentence using a vocabulary word.

1. Use the word *malediction* in a sentence about a character in a story or a fairy tale.

   Sample Answer: The witch angrily delivered her male-

   diction: The baby would one day prick his finger on a

   thorn and die.

2. Describe the behavior of an irritating salesperson. Use the word *loquacious*.

   Sample Answer: Once the loquacious salesperson got

   started, it was impossible to escape his constant chatter.

3. Use the word *circumlocution* to describe how someone responded to a question.

   Sample Answer: Not knowing the answer to the teacher's

   question, Jenny engaged in a pattern of circumlocution,

   hoping to "land" on the right answer.

4. Complete the following sentence: I stated that the meeting was scheduled for Tuesday evening, but Klaus *contradicted* me by saying . . .

   Sample Answer: I stated that the meeting was scheduled

   for Tuesday evening, but Klaus contradicted me by say-

   ing the meeting had been canceled.

Decide which word in parentheses best completes the sentence. Then write the sentence, adding the missing word.

5. The university is sponsoring a _____ on American foreign policy in Asia. (colloquium; dictum)

   colloquium

6. I will _____ the words, and you will write them in your notebook. (dictate, interdict)

   dictate

7. The king issued a(n) _____ honoring Robin Hood and all his
   followers. (edict; malediction)

   edict _____

   _____

8. Lincoln was not known for his _____, so Edward Everett was
   asked to give the main speech at Gettysburg. (colloquium; elocution)

   elocution _____

   _____

9. The drug enforcement agencies play an important role in ____ the
   entry of illegal drugs into the country. (dictating; interdicting)

   interdicting _____

   _____

10. My boss is so pompous that he doesn't write a memo, he issues a
    _____. (circumlocution; dictum)

    dictum _____

    _____

Test-Taking Strategies

An antonym test asks you to choose the word that is most nearly <u>opposite</u>
in meaning to another word.

Sample

S. SWEET	(A) simple	(B) angry	S. _____C_____
	(C) sour	(D) large	

Because this test asks you to distinguish between words with slightly different meanings, it is good to look at all the choices before answering. Also,
be careful <u>not</u> to choose a synonym as your answer.

Practice: Choose the word or phrase that is most nearly <u>opposite</u> in meaning to the word in capital letters.

| 1. MALEDICTION | (A) curse | (B) quiet reflection | 1. ____C____ |
| | (C) blessing | (D) friendliness | |

| 2. CONSUME | (A) release | (B) conserve | 2. ____B____ |
| | (C) admire | (D) refuse | |

| 3. APATHY | (A) morality | (B) luxury | 3. ____C____ |
| | (C) enthusiasm | (D) danger | |

How well do you remember the words you studied in Lessons 16 through 18? Take the following test covering the words from the last three lessons.

Part 1 Antonyms

Each question below includes a word in capital letters, followed by four words or phrases. Choose the word or phrase that is most nearly <u>opposite</u> in meaning to the word in capital letters. Consider all choices before deciding on your answer. Write the letter for your answer on the line provided.

S. HIGH	(A) cold	(B) simple	**S.**	**C**
	(C) low	(D) foolish		

1. RIGOROUS	(A) disciplined	(B) casual	**1.**	**B**
	(C) ordinary	(D) pleasant		
2. MALEDICTION	(A) compliment	(B) summary	**2.**	**A**
	(C) perfume	(D) awkwardness		
3. CIRCUMLOCUTION	(A) circular arrangement	(B) direct statement	**3.**	**B**
	(C) triangular	(D) confusing message		
4. DERIDE	(A) to climb upon	(B) to ridicule	**4.**	**D**
	(C) to fasten firmly	(D) to praise		
5. UPBRAID	(A) to denounce	(B) to decorate	**5.**	**C**
	(C) to approve	(D) to clarify		
6. SUCCULENT	(A) edible	(B) parched	**6.**	**B**
	(C) generous	(D) mature		
7. CONTRADICT	(A) to revise	(B) to allow easy passage	**7.**	**C**
	(C) to accept willingly	(D) to provoke		
8. AMELIORATE	(A) to make worse	(B) to forgive	**8.**	**A**
	(C) to change one's mind frequently	(D) to study in depth		
9. INTERDICT	(A) to interrupt	(B) to judge harshly	**9.**	**D**
	(C) to cause great sorrow	(D) to permit passage		

Go on to next page. ➤

10. ASPERSION   (A) flattery   (B) secret opinion   10. _____ **A** _____
                     (C) important event   (D) lack of ambition

Part 2 Matching Words and Meanings

Match the definition in Column B with the word in Column A. Write the letter of the correct definition on the line provided

Column A	Column B	
11. censure	a. the art of public speaking	11. _____ h _____
12. prudent	b. place to get food and supplies	12. _____ c _____
13. innuendo	c. wise and careful	13. _____ l _____
14. critique	d. type of conference or meeting	14. _____ n _____
15. tawny	e. an order or command	15. _____ f _____
16. acrimonious	f. golden brown	16. _____ m _____
17. dictate	g. agricultural	17. _____ e _____
18. defame	h. formal act of disapproval	18. _____ j _____
19. elocution	i. to cut out	19. _____ a _____
20. colloquium	j. to slander	20. _____ d _____
21. gambol	k. to discredit	21. _____ o _____
22. commissary	l. indirect or subtle suggestion of wrongdoing	22. _____ b _____
23. impeach	m. bitterly hostile	23. _____ k _____
24. excise	n. an analysis	24. _____ i _____
25. agrarian	o. to frolic playfully	25. _____ g _____

Name _____

The Language of Sign

When American Sign Language (ASL) was introduced in the early 1800s, it was regarded as no more than a form of **pidgin** English. However, it differed from other forms of pidgin English in that it consisted of a combination of gestures that looked like the ideas or words the gestures were
5 supposed to represent. Assuming that language must be based on speech or modulations of sound, **linguists** regarded as **heresy** the notion that signed languages are natural languages like English, French, and Chinese. In the past twenty years, however, linguists have acknowledged that signed languages like ASL are as powerful and intricately structured as
10 spoken ones, and that they are capable of expressing the **subtle** shades of meaning possible with spoken languages.

Just as speakers combine meaningless bits of sound into meaningful words, signers unite individually meaningless hand and body movements into words. They choose from a **palette** of assorted hand shapes, such as a fist or
15 a pointed index finger. They also choose where to make a sign and how to **orient** the hand and the arm. Each shape and position provides context clues to the intended meaning. Furthermore, ASL has a key language ingredient: a grammar to regulate its flow. For example, a signer might make the sign for "Jane" at some point in space. By pointing to that spot later, the signer
20 creates the pronoun *she* or *her*, meaning Jane. A sign moving toward the spot means something done *to* her; a sign moving away from the spot means an action done *by* her. Facial expressions and head movements also function as grammatical markers, providing **crucial** linguistic information. A head tilted forward and raised eyebrows, for instance, turn a statement into a question.

25 This complex system of gestures sheds new light on the old scientific controversy over whether language is an **innate** human instinct or learned behavior. Linguists have reasoned that if ASL is a true language, unconnected to speech, then our **proclivity** for language must be built in at birth, whether we express it with our tongue or with our hands. The work
30 of research psychologists supports this belief; deaf babies of deaf parents babble in sign. Just as hearing infants create nonsense sounds as their first attempts at language, so, too, do deaf babies, but they do so with their hands. Their systematic hand and finger movements, totally unlike those of hearing children, are a way of exploring the linguistic units that will be
35 the building blocks of their language.

Like any living language, ASL is **dynamic** and continues to evolve. For example, terms that were visual representations of ethnic stereotypes have been replaced by finely tuned, sensitized signs. The language of sign is hardly silent; instead, it is alive with unique patterns that communicate
40 meaning.

Words
crucial
dynamic
heresy
innate
linguist
orient
palette
pidgin
proclivity
subtle

Unlocking Meaning

Each word in this lesson's word list appears in dark type in the selection you just read. Think about how the vocabulary word is used in the selection, then write the letter for the best answer to each question.

1. In line 2 *pidgin* means ____.
   (A) modern
   (B) a tendency to spread
   (C) a simplified blend of languages
   (D) dependent on birds

   1. **C**

2. *Linguists* (line 6) can best be described as ____.
   (A) people who study language
   (B) historians
   (C) diplomats
   (D) computer operators

   2. **A**

3. Which words could best replace *heresy* in line 6?
   (A) a brilliant discovery
   (B) an opinion opposed to established views
   (C) scientifically accurate
   (D) a logical conclusion

   3. **B**

4. *Subtle* (line 10) shades of meaning ____.
   (A) are difficult to detect
   (B) have a smooth surface
   (C) deviate from the normal
   (D) are immediately obvious

   4. **A**

5. A *palette* (line 14) can best be explained as a ____.
   (A) mysterious arrangement
   (B) short essay
   (C) style of writing
   (D) range of choices

   5. **D**

6. Which words could best replace *orient* in line 16?
   (A) mold with precision
   (B) distribute widely
   (C) align or position
   (D) bear the weight of

   6. **C**

7. Which word or words could best replace *crucial* in line 23?
   (A) unimportant
   (B) extremely significant
   (C) low in rank
   (D) lacking energy

   7. **B**

8. In line 26, *innate* means ____.
   (A) connected by links
   (B) possessed at birth
   (C) unnoticed
   (D) repetitive

   8. **B**

9. A *proclivity* (line 28) can best be explained as ____.
   (A) a natural tendency
   (B) a dislike
   (C) an inability to master
   (D) a deficiency

   9. **A**

10. Which word or words could best replace *dynamic* in line 36?
    (A) peculiar
    (B) extremely loud
    (C) tending to hold persistently to something
    (D) characterized by continuous change or activity

    10. **D**

Name _____

Applying Meaning

Decide which word in parentheses best completes the sentence. Then write the sentence, adding the missing word.

1. A _____ for fainting at the sight of blood would not be desirable for someone interested in a medical career. (heresy; proclivity)

   proclivity _____

   _____

   _____

2. The Grimm brothers were not only collectors of fairy tales, they were also pioneers of modern _____ with their *German Dictionary*. (linguistics; palettes)

   linguistics _____

   _____

   _____

3. The copies of the famous painting easily fooled the uninformed buyers, but the art expert found some _____ differences between the copies and the original. (dynamic; subtle)

   subtle _____

   _____

   _____

4. Combining English, Portuguese, German, Bengali, French, and Malayan, the _____ English developed by British traders in China takes its name from the way the Chinese pronounced *business*—"bijin." (innate; pidgin)

   pidgin _____

   _____

   _____

5. Katharine Hepburn's _____ personality coupled with her colorful stories about those she worked with make the actress a fascinating subject for an interview. (crucial; dynamic)

   dynamic _____

   _____

   _____

Read each sentence below. Write "correct" on the answer line if the vocabulary word has been used correctly. Write "incorrect" on the answer line if the vocabulary word has been used incorrectly.

6. Hector is my pal, and Judy is my *palette*.

6. __incorrect__

7. When you are attempting to find your way with a map and compass, the first step is to *orient* yourself to a recognizable point on the map and determine which way is north.

7. __correct__

8. Because of his rejection of the established beliefs of the Roman Catholic church, Martin Luther was charged with *heresy*.

8. __correct__

9. All of us were embarrassed by Roger's *innate* remarks during the meeting.

9. __incorrect__

10. The polka is a *crucial* and lively dance that originated in eastern Europe and was introduced in the United States by immigrants.

10. __incorrect__

For each word used incorrectly, write a sentence using the word properly.

Answers will vary.

_____

_____

_____

_____

_____

_____

_____

_____

_____

_____

_____

_____

_____

Mastering Meaning

Look for information on a type of pidgin English used somewhere in the world. Write a report on some element of its vocabulary or grammar and on how pidgin English is useful in helping certain people communicate. Use some of the words you studied in this lesson.

Lesson 20 **Part A**

Name _____

People who are interested in a particular subject, whether it be carpentry, nuclear physics, or gardening, use a specialized vocabulary to discuss that subject with others. While a casual observer might call any boat with a sail a sailboat, an experienced sailor will refer to sloops, yawls, and ketches. Art and music are similar specialties, each with its own vocabulary. In this lesson you will study ten words from the fields of art and music.

Unlocking Meaning

Read the sentences or short passages below. Write the letter for the correct definition of the italicized vocabulary word.

In the quiet of the summer evening, we enjoyed the *dulcet* tones of the church choir as it practiced several hymns.

1. (A) harsh and grating
   (B) sweet and melodious
   (C) distressing
   (D) unwelcome

The story of a man who sells his soul to the devil for worldly gain is a common *motif* in the literature of many nations. In American literature, it occurs in Washington Irving's "The Devil and Tom Walker." In German literature, it is found in Goethe's *Faust*.

2. (A) song
   (B) surprise ending
   (C) historical event
   (D) recurring idea or theme

The realistic landscapes and portraits exhibited in the art museum stood in sharp contrast to the *abstract* paintings being sold on the street corner. Looking at those blobs of paint and geometric figures, I was tempted to ask the artist, "What is it?"

3. (A) not tied to anything practical or concrete
   (B) meaningful
   (C) literal
   (D) easily understood

Members of the *avant-garde* in any field always run the risk of being ridiculed or ignored. Not many years ago, Paul Gauguin's colorful paintings of Polynesian scenes were thought to be shocking and repulsive. Now, he is considered one of the most important influences on modern art.

4. (A) experts
   (B) immoral influences
   (C) people who try out new ideas
   (D) scholars

Words

a cappella

abstract

aesthetic

avant-garde

cacophony

dissonance

dulcet

libretto

motif

surrealistic

1. _____**B**_____

2. _____**D**_____

3. _____**A**_____

4. _____**C**_____

The choir preferred to sing the selections *a cappella*. The singers felt that the addition of instruments would overwhelm their subtle vocal sounds.

5. (A) electronically enhanced
   (B) without instrumental accompaniment
   (C) in a slow, serious manner
   (D) with little rehearsal

5. _____**B**_____

Before orchestra practice begins, each musician tunes his or her instrument by playing a random series of notes. The result is a *cacophony* of horns, drums, and stringed instruments that makes you want to cover your ears.

6. (A) melodious blend
   (B) sudden, quiet pause
   (C) musical composition
   (D) harsh, jarring sound

6. _____**D**_____

The director began the meeting by giving a copy of the *libretto* to each member of the cast. The performers would spend days studying every element of this complex opera before attempting to rehearse it onstage.

7. (A) text of a dramatic musical work
   (B) seating chart for a theater
   (C) list of complaints
   (D) rules for behavior

7. _____**A**_____

With its clever use of glass and steel, the office building was an *aesthetic* masterpiece. Unfortunately, however, there was little available parking space and no public transportation. Without these more practical requirements, the building would never be used to its capacity.

8. (A) frequently imitated
   (B) artistic
   (C) profitable
   (D) inexpensive

8. _____**B**_____

Melting clocks, fantastic animals, nightmarish phantoms, and similar *surrealistic* images are found in the works of several modern artists.

9. (A) illogical, dreamlike
   (B) humorous
   (C) highly detailed
   (D) pleasingly colorful

9. _____**A**_____

The conductor of the orchestra possessed an exceptionally keen ear. She could detect the slightest *dissonance* and identify the musician responsible for the problem.

10. (A) lack of attention
    (B) misbehavior
    (C) lack of harmony
    (D) improved performance

10. _____**C**_____

Applying Meaning

Decide which word(s) in parentheses best complete(s) the sentence. Then write the sentence, adding the missing word(s).

1. Since everyone claimed to see something different in each painting, the exhibit of ____ art generated a great deal of controversy. (a cappella; abstract)

   abstract _____

   _____

   _____

2. The professor felt Amal lacked the ____ appreciation needed to be successful and suggested that Amal consider dropping out of art school. (aesthetic; surrealistic)

   aesthetic _____

   _____

   _____

3. Most critics disliked the work of the new artist intensely, but a few felt she was in the ____ of a new and important style. (avant-garde; motif)

   avant-garde _____

   _____

   _____

4. After seeing the band receive a standing ovation for its performance, I found it unlikely that just six months ago the only sound it could produce was a ____ of confusion. (cacophony; dulcet)

   cacophony _____

   _____

   _____

5. The Bible is the source of many literary ____, such as the story of Cain and Abel. (librettos; motifs)

   motifs _____

   _____

   _____

Each question below contains a vocabulary word from this lesson. Answer each question "yes" or "no" in the space provided.

6. If you wanted to be reminded of the exact appearance of a dear friend, would you ask a *surrealistic* artist to paint a picture of him?

   6. ____ **no** ____

7. Would a skillful violinist want to produce *dulcet* music for an audience?

   7. ____ **yes** ____

8. Does an *a cappella* quartet require the services of a piano tuner?

8. _____no_____

9. Would the artistic director of an opera need a *libretto* to do a proper job?

9. _____yes_____

10. Do museums usually employ members of the *avant-garde* as security officers?

10. _____no_____

11. Would a music critic be pleased to hear *dissonant* sounds during a performance of "The Sound of Music"?

11. _____no_____

12. Should a successful work of art be *aesthetically* pleasing?

12. _____yes_____

For each question you answered "no," write a sentence using the vocabulary word correctly.

Answers will vary.

_____

_____

_____

_____

_____

_____

_____

_____

_____

_____

_____

Bonus Word

mobile

A *mobile* (pronounced mō′bēl′) is a type of modern sculpture made up of carefully balanced parts, hanging from a central strand, that move in response to air currents. A mobile often uses abstract shapes and colorful designs that reconfigure themselves as they turn slowly in the air. The adjective *mobile* (pronounced mō′bəl, mō′bēl′, or mō′bīl′) however, means "capable of being moved." The same word spelled with a capital letter and pronounced mō′bēl′ or mō′bēl′ is the name of a city in southwestern Alabama.

Write a Critique: Alexander Calder created a number of interesting mobiles. Find a picture of one of his mobiles in an art reference book and write a critique of its artistic merit. Use some of the words you studied in this lesson.

The Roots -voc- and -clam-

Name _____

The Latin word for "to call" is *vocare*. It usually appears as *-voc-* in English words, but occasionally it appears as *-vok-* or even *-vouc-*. Most English words with this root still keep some element of "call" in their meaning. The Latin word *clamare* means "to cry out." English words with this root usually keep some part of this original Latin meaning. This root appears as *-clam-* or *-claim-*. Each vocabulary word in this lesson has one of these two roots.

Root	Meaning	English Word
-voc-	to call	avocation
-vok-		revoke
-vouc-		vouch
-clam-	to cry out	proclamation
-claim-		claimant

Words

- avocation
- claimant
- clamorous
- declaim
- equivocate
- evocative
- irrevocable
- proclamation
- reclamation
- vouch

Unlocking Meaning

Write the vocabulary word that fits each clue below. Then say the word and write a short definition. Compare your definition and pronunciation with those given on the flash card.

1. This word is the adjective form of "evoke." It combines the prefix *e-*, meaning "out," with the root we get from the Latin word *vocare*.

   evocative. Definitions will vary.
   _____
   _____

2. This word is the noun form for "proclaim." It combines the prefix *pro-*, meaning "forward," with the root we get from the Latin word *clamare*. Abraham Lincoln issued one of these to free the slaves.

   proclamation. Definitions will vary.
   _____
   _____

3. This word has the *-ant* ending, meaning "one who does something." What this person might do is cry out, "That belongs to me!"

   claimant. Definitions will vary.
   _____
   _____

4. The "call" root is joined with the *a-* prefix, meaning "away." In a sense, this word calls you away from work and other required duties.

avocation. Definitions will vary.

5. This verb has an unusual spelling for the "call" root. It is something you might do for a friend who needs to prove his or her honesty.

vouch. Definitions will vary.

6. You will find the *-equi-* root, meaning "fair" or "equal," in this verb. It might apply to someone who cannot make up his or her mind.

equivocate. Definitions will vary.

7. This adjective comes from the noun *clamor*, a loud, continuous noise. It suggests that the noise is a crying out of some kind.

clamorous. Definitions will vary.

8. This adjective begins with two prefixes: the *ir-* prefix, meaning "not," and the *re-* prefix, meaning "again" or "back."

irrevocable. Definitions will vary.

9. This word is the verb form of *declamation*, meaning "a strong, forceful speech." It came from the Middle English word *declamen*.

declaim. Definitions will vary.

10. This noun combines the *re-* prefix, meaning "again," with the call root. You might recognize this as a form of the word "reclaim."

reclamation. Definitions will vary.

Name _____

Applying Meaning

Follow the directions below to write a sentence using a vocabulary word.

1. Tell about something you do on weekends. Use the word *avocation*.

Sample Answer: On weekends I pursue my avocation of hang-gliding.

2. Tell about a difficult decision. Use any form of the word *equivocate*.

Sample Answer: After weeks of equivocation, I decided to accept the part-time job at Vandy's Grocery Store.

3. Describe the welcome a rock star might receive. Use the word *clamorous*.

Sample Answer: A clamorous crowd poured through the airport lobby as The Green Machine's plane taxied to the gate.

4. Write a sentence that would help a friend get a job. Use the word *vouch*.

Sample Answer: I can vouch for the honesty and dependability of my friend Françoise LeFleur.

5. Write a one-sentence announcement to tell the winner of a contest how to go about getting his or her prize. Use the word *claimant*.

Sample Answer: After the winner of the drawing is announced, the claimant should bring the winning ticket to the contest headquarters.

Decide which word in parentheses best completes the sentence. Then write the sentence, adding the missing word.

6. The smell of freshly baked bread was _____ of the happy days I spent at Grandmother's house years ago. (evocative; irrevocable)

evocative

---

7. We pleaded with Ms. Jarvis to give us an extra day to complete the assigned work, but her decision was ____ . (evocative; irrevocable)

irrevocable

_____

_____

8. The city began a huge ____ project designed to collect and recycle newspapers and glass bottles. (proclamation; reclamation)

reclamation

_____

_____

9. The angry citizen spent twenty minutes at the meeting of the city council ____ about the poor garbage collection. (declaiming; equivocating)

declaiming

_____

_____

10. In honor of the high school football team's great season, the superintendent issued a formal ____ naming Friday Panther Pride Day. (avocation; proclamation)

proclamation

_____

_____

●	*Cultural Literacy Note*
	red herring
	Red herring are fish that have a strong odor when they are cured by salting. The odor is so strong, in fact, that if a red herring is dragged across the trail of an animal being chased by hunting dogs, the dogs will become confused and begin following the trail of the herring. Consequently, *red herring* has come to refer to any deliberate distraction, especially in an argument. Calling someone a socialist in a debate over taxes might be considered a red herring.
	Cooperative Learning: Work with a partner to prepare a short debate or discussion on a subject of interest to the class. In your prepared remarks include a few red herrings. Read your remarks to the class to see if anyone can catch the red herrings.

How well do you remember the words you studied in Lessons 19 through 21? Take the following test covering the words from the last three lessons.

Part 1 Antonyms

Each question below includes a word in capital letters, followed by four words or phrases. Choose the word or phrase that is most nearly <u>opposite</u> in meaning to the word in capital letters. Consider all choices before deciding on your answer. Write the letter for your answer on the line provided.

Sample

S. GOOD	(A) simple	(B) bad	S. **B**
	(C) able	(D) fast	

1. IRREVOCABLE	(A) simple	(B) revisable	1. **B**
	(C) unchangeable	(D) serious	

2. ABSTRACT	(A) concrete	(B) invisible	2. **A**
	(C) combined	(D) absent-minded	

3. INNATE	(A) imprisoned	(B) knowledgeable	3. **C**
	(C) acquired	(D) joyful	

4. SUBTLE	(A) superior	(B) obvious	4. **B**
	(C) unknown	(D) bland	

5. AVANT-GARDE	(A) guardian	(B) harsh noises	5. **D**
	(C) threatening gesture	(D) conservatives	

6. CRUCIAL	(A) unplanned	(B) temporary	6. **C**
	(C) unimportant	(D) desirable	

7. EQUIVOCATE	(A) penalize	(B) remove	7. **C**
	(C) resolve	(D) destroy	

8. DULCET	(A) brilliant	(B) admired	8. **D**
	(C) angry	(D) grating	

9. DYNAMIC	(A) changeless	(B) mechanical	9. **A**
	(C) unnecessary	(D) frequent	

Go on to next page. ➤

10. AVOCATION   (A) pleasure trip   (B) reversal   **10.** _____ **D** _____
                   (C) solemn promise   (D) unpleasant chore

11. VOUCH   (A) promise   (B) harm   **11.** _____ **D** _____
               (C) dismiss   (D) deny

12. CACOPHONY   (A) harmonious sound   (B) complex musical   **12.** _____ **A** _____
                                                       composition
                     (C) poor imitation   (D) artistic success

13. HERESY   (A) foolish remark   (B) accepted belief   **13.** _____ **B** _____
               (C) convincing   (D) unpopular idea
                       argument

14. CLAMOROUS   (A) lovable   (B) confusing   **14.** _____ **C** _____
                     (C) peaceful   (D) unclaimed

15. DISSONANCE   (A) melodious sounds   (B) source of support   **15.** _____ **A** _____
                     (C) legal acceptance   (D) careful plan

Part 2 Matching Words and Meanings

Match the definition in Column B with the word in Column A.
Write the letter of the correct definition on the answer line.

Column A	Column B		
16. orient	a. without instrumental accompaniment	**16.**	b
17. motif	b. to position or place	**17.**	f
18. declaim	c. speak loudly and forcefully	**18.**	c
19. proclamation	d. dreamlike	**19.**	g
20. pidgin	e. able to call forth	**20.**	i
21. proclivity	f. repeated theme	**21.**	j
22. a cappella	g. official announcement	**22.**	a
23. evocative	h. expert on language	**23.**	e
24. surrealistic	i. mixture of languages	**24.**	d
25. linguist	j. tendency	**25.**	h

Name _____

Playing Your Cards Right

It's a peaceful summer afternoon in the late 1950s, and sounds of Elvis
Presley and Buddy Holly wail from almost-new portable radios. In yards
and on street corners, young boys—and maybe a few girls—take packs of
rubber-banded cards from their pockets. Flipping thin cardboard in reg-
5 ular competitions, they maintain a **steadfast** hope of winning a Willie
Mays or a Mickey Mantle from an **unwary** friend. Today, those same boys
and girls have grown up, and they **plumb** attics and basements for the
shoeboxes that housed their baseball cards. Once the pastime of grade-
school kids, collecting baseball cards has become big business, and glee-
10 ful hobbyists have been **transfigured** into serious-minded investors.

The first mass-produced baseball cards were issued in the 1880s. They were
sold with everything from gum to dog food. The publishers' **inchoate**
notions of what the cards should contain seem rather peculiar today.
These early cards bore little resemblance to current laser-printed col-
15 lectibles. Lacking biography or statistics on the back, they sported only a
studio photograph of a player swinging at a ball suspended on a string.

These earliest cards are not as valuable as most people think. With only a
few exceptions, yesterday's players fall short of both the flashiness and the
records of more current stars. Furthermore, although the early cards meet
20 the demands of age and rarity, they usually lack an important **variable** in
determining worth—condition. **Pristine** cards are straight-out-of-the-
package perfect: sharp corners, crisp edges, and brilliant colors. Even the
tiniest defect **indelibly** labels a card as damaged goods. A card handled
but not abused commands only 20 to 30 percent of the price of one in
25 mint condition. Shoeboxes have given way to specially designed holders
that offer protection from the elements.

Although governed by laws of supply and demand, the business of collecting is very complicated. The star quality of the player has to be factored in.
As collectors and dealers **vie** for choice merchandise, they speculate on play-
30 ers' futures. Rookie cards of players who were later elected to the Hall of
Fame are thus among the most valuable. The cards of power hitters do better than those of other players. Pitchers are the biggest risk of all, because
they are always in danger of career-threatening arm injuries. Originally a simple hobby with few rules, baseball-card collecting and investing today de-
35 pend on monthly price guides, computer programs, and dealer shows.

Putting money into baseball cards is **akin** to speculating on the stock market. There is no guarantee that the investment will maintain even a faint
reflection of the cost. Baseball-card enthusiasts agree, however, that it is
better to be stuck with a collection of their favorite heroes than with a
40 bunch of equally worthless stock certificates.

Words
akin
inchoate
indelible
plumb
pristine
steadfast
transfigure
unwary
variable
vie

Unlocking Meaning

Each word in this lesson's word list appears in dark type in the selection you just read. Think about how the vocabulary word is used in the selection, then write the letter for the best answer to each question.

1. Which word or words could best replace *steadfast* in line 5?
   (A) halfhearted   (B) unnecessary
   (C) steady   (D) disorderly

   1. _____C_____

2. Someone who is *unwary* (line 6) could best be described as _____.
   (A) lacking caution   (B) forgetful
   (C) careful   (D) disorganized

   2. _____A_____

3. Which word or words could best replace *plumb* in line 7?
   (A) escape from   (B) measure
   (C) treat thoughtlessly (D) examine closely

   3. _____D_____

4. Which word or words could best replace *transfigured* in line 10?
   (A) changed   (B) consumed carelessly
   (C) affected negatively (D) separated

   4. _____A_____

5. If something is *inchoate* (line 12), it can best be described as _____.
   (A) easily irritated   (B) in an early stage
   (C) geographically close (D) random

   5. _____B_____

6. A *variable* (line 20) can best be described as _____.
   (A) a pattern of markings   (B) a member of a group
   (C) something likely to change (D) one of a series

   6. _____C_____

7. Which word could best replace *Pristine* in line 21?
   (A) Modest   (B) Incidental
   (C) Remarkable   (D) Unspoiled

   7. _____D_____

8. Which word could best replace *indelibly* in line 23?
   (A) privately   (B) permanently
   (C) without equal   (D) unfairly

   8. _____B_____

9. Which words could best replace *vie* in line 29?
   (A) live lavishly   (B) cause to appear greater
   (C) make note of   (D) strive for superiority

   9. _____D_____

10. *Akin* (line 36) can best be explained as _____.
    (A) having a similar character (B) not openly practiced
    (C) winning approval   (D) excessively sentimental

   10. _____A_____

Applying Meaning

Follow the directions below to write a sentence using a vocabulary word.

1. Describe a tourist who is not used to crowded city streets. Use a form of the word *unwary*.

   Sample Answer: Unfamiliar with the law allowing a right turn on red, the unwary tourist was almost hit by a taxi as she crossed the street.

2. Explain how someone might go about memorizing the words to a song or a poem. Use a form of the word *indelible*.

   Sample Answer: With only one tape for the entire ten-hour trip, Carlo would have the song lyrics indelibly etched in his memory.

3. Describe something that has been kept in a safe place for a long time. Use a form of the word *pristine*.

   Sample Answer: Because I have kept it wrapped in a soft cloth for years, the silver dollar I received on my first birthday is still in pristine condition.

4. Make a comparison between two difficult tasks. Use the word *akin*.

   Sample Answer: Trying to win an argument with my brother is akin to forcing an independent cat to curl up in one's lap for a nap.

5. Describe someone's behavior or attitude toward an environmental issue. Use a form of the word *steadfast*.

   Sample Answer: Regardless of where she has lived, Ms. Chen has steadfastly defended the plight of abandoned house pets.

Each question below contains a vocabulary word from this lesson. Answer each question "yes" or "no" in the space provided.

6. Can someone *plumb* his or her memory for a familiar name or face?   6. _____ **yes** _____

7. Is an *inchoate* plan nearly finished?   7. _____ **no** _____

8. Is a *variable* a statement or plan suggested for acceptance?   8. _____ **no** _____

9. Can a person's appearance be *transfigured* by a new haircut or different eyeglasses?

9. _____**yes**_____

10. If a book makes it to the top of the best-seller list, can it be said to have *vied* successfully for that position?

10. _____**yes**_____

11. Could a sleeping rabbit be an *unwary* victim of a hunter?

11. _____**yes**_____

12. Can a football coach declare a player *indelible* to play in a game because of an injury?

12. _____**no**_____

For each question you answered "no," write a sentence using the vocabulary word correctly.

Answers will vary.

_____

_____

_____

_____

_____

_____

_____

_____

_____

_____

_____

_____

_____

_____

Mastering Meaning

Have you ever noticed that places you visited as a child seem very different when you return as a teenager? Whether it's because of your physical and emotional maturity, or simple recall, certain locations seem smaller and less exciting after the passage of years. Choose a particular place, such as an amusement park, a friend's or relative's back yard, or a restaurant, and write a comparison and contrast essay. In your description, show how the place has changed. Use some of the words you studied in this lesson.

Name _____

People often have a way of going too far with something, so it is not surprising that the English language has a number of words to reflect the concepts of greed and excess. In this lesson you will study ten words associated with this human habit of going too far.

Unlocking Meaning

Read the sentences or short passages below. Write the letter for the correct definition of the italicized vocabulary word.

Captain Ahab was *obsessed* with killing the white whale Moby Dick. He abandoned all other interests in this blind pursuit that eventually cost many lives.

1. (A) excessively preoccupied
    (B) mildly interested
    (C) disgusted
    (D) entertained

Joseph Conrad's *Heart of Darkness* tells of the unchecked *rapacity* of European ivory traders in Africa. Traders who originally entered the jungle with good intentions ended up enslaving or murdering the native population for the sake of stealing more and more ivory.

2. (A) humanity
    (B) religious feelings
    (C) willingness to take what one wants by force
    (D) tendency to commit small injustices

First Sean shoved an entire sandwich in his mouth. Then he washed it down with a quart of milk and a pint of ice cream. Such *gluttonous* behavior might be acceptable for someone who has not eaten for days, but Sean had eaten breakfast just an hour before.

3. (A) lovable
    (B) greedy about food and drink
    (C) childish
    (D) dangerous

After the radio station offered free rock-concert tickets to the first one hundred callers, the switchboard was *inundated* with calls. Even after the station announced that all the tickets were gone, the calls continued for hours.

4. (A) annoyed
    (B) deceived
    (C) embarrassed
    (D) flooded

Words
avarice
gluttonous
intemperate
inundate
obsess
parsimony
prodigal
profligate
rapacity
replete

1. _____**A**_____

2. _____**C**_____

3. _____**B**_____

4. _____**D**_____

When the owner's *profligate* son took over the business, he bought a new office building, put all his friends on the payroll, hired a chauffeur to drive him around in a limousine, and took several long vacations. The business went bankrupt in six months.

5. (A) recklessly wasteful
   (B) clever
   (C) excessively careful
   (D) popular

5. _____A_____

The landlord, motivated by pure *avarice* in dealing with tenants, constantly raised the rents and absolutely refused to make any repairs on the shabby apartments.

6. (A) strict morality
   (B) secret desires
   (C) strong desire for wealth
   (D) concern for the less fortunate

6. _____C_____

In Charles Dickens's *A Christmas Carol*, Mr. Scrooge is portrayed as the embodiment of *parsimony*. He pays his employees as little as possible and resents giving them time off, even for Christmas.

7. (A) generosity
   (B) holiday spirit
   (C) ignorance about money matters
   (D) stinginess

7. _____D_____

From a distance the swamp looked quiet enough, but in reality it was *replete* with mosquitoes, alligators, and every imaginable kind of snake.

8. (A) filled to abundance
   (B) decorated
   (C) designed
   (D) enlarged

8. _____A_____

Jake regretted the *intemperate* words he had spoken to his mother that morning. There was simply no excuse for yelling such things at someone who was only trying to help.

9. (A) confusing
   (B) strong and unrestrained
   (C) kind and gentle
   (D) wise and intelligent

9. _____B_____

The remorse of a *prodigal* child is a favorite theme in literature. In such stories, a parent welcomes home a long-lost son or daughter who has spent his or her inheritance foolishly. Meanwhile, the other children, who have faithfully remained at home, feel they are being slighted.

10. (A) industrious
    (B) curious
    (C) elderly
    (D) recklessly extravagant

10. _____D_____

Applying Meaning

Follow the directions below to write a sentence using a vocabulary word.

1. Write a sentence telling about an important goal you or someone you know would like to achieve. Use any form of the word *obsess*.

   Sample Answer: Alicia is obsessed with the idea of becoming a pilot in the United States Air Force.

   _____

2. Use the word *intemperate* to describe something you or someone you know said or did.

   Sample Answer: Running onto the football field to argue with the referee was the most intemperate thing I have ever seen Coach Robinson do.

3. Describe the behavior of someone at a picnic. Use any form of the word *gluttonous*.

   Sample Answer: After playing in the hot sun for an hour, Sergi acted like a complete glutton at the picnic table by drinking a pitcher of lemonade and eating six hot dogs.

4. Use the word *avarice* or *avaricious* to describe something that someone you have read about has done.

   Sample Answer: King Midas's avaricious desire to have everything he touched turn to gold proved to be a curse.

   _____

5. Describe what might happen to a sports hero who offered a free autographed picture to anyone who made a donation to his favorite charity. Use any form of the word *inundate*.

   Sample Answer: After Lefty Blanchard's announcement, the Homeless Relief Foundation was inundated with donations.

6. Write a sentence about someone who changed from behaving in an evil or wicked way to always doing good. Use the word *profligate*.

   Sample Answer: After her close call with death, Karen changed her profligate ways and began to do volunteer work at the shelter.

Decide which word in parentheses best completes the sentence. Then write the sentence, adding the missing word.

7. Thanks to a vigorous conservation program, the once-dead lake is now _____ with trout and other game fish. (gluttonous; replete)

   replete _____

   _____

   _____

8. The _____ owner planned to charge his employees for the water they drank from the company drinking fountain. (parsimonious; profligate)

   parsimonious _____

   _____

   _____

9. Thanks to the _____ policies of the treasurer over the past four years, the city is now out of money and must again raise taxes. (parsimonious; prodigal)

   prodigal _____

   _____

   _____

10. After rioting soldiers took the cultural treasures from the museum, the United Nations condemned the _____ actions of the conquering country. (obsessive; rapacious)

    rapacious _____

    _____

    _____

	Cultural Literacy Note
●	**A Wolf in Sheep's Clothing**
	One of Aesop's many fables tells of a wolf's attempt to steal sheep by
	disguising itself in a sheepskin and slipping into a pasture among the
	other animals. That night the shepherd unknowingly pens the wolf in
	with his sheep. Later, the shepherd decides to slaughter one of the
	sheep for dinner, and you can guess which one he selects. Because of
	this popular story, the expression "wolf in sheep's clothing" has come to
	refer to someone threatening disguised as someone kind.
	Write a Paragraph: Explain something someone did that you feel quali-
	fies that person to be called a wolf in sheep's clothing.

Lesson
24
Part A

Name _____

Whether we like it or not, death, pain, and disease are part of life. Three Latin words have provided us with a number of roots for words in this rather unhappy area of experience. The Latin word *mort,* meaning "death," can be seen easily in an English word like *immortalize,* but it is not so apparent in *mortgage.* The Latin *mordere,* meaning "to bite," occurs in English words related to painful experiences, such as *remorse.* The Latin *morbus* means "disease," and can be found in the English word *morbid.* Each of the vocabulary words in this lesson has one of these Latin roots.

Root	Meaning	English Word
-mort-	death	immortalize
-mord- -mor-	bite	mordant remorse
-morb-	disease	morbid

Unlocking Meaning

A vocabulary word appears in italics in each sentence or short passage below. Find the root in the vocabulary word and think about how the word is used in the passage. Then write a definition for the vocabulary word. Compare your definition with the definition on the flash card.

1. Traffic was backed up for miles because people were slowing down to watch the injured being removed from cars involved in an accident. Such *morbid* curiosity seems to be growing in our culture.
   Definitions will vary.
   _____
   _____

2. The homebuyer had a good job and a steady income, so the bank agreed to lend her the money. However, if this *mortgage* was not paid regularly for the next twenty years, the bank would take the house.
   Definitions will vary.
   _____
   _____

3. The homebuyer decided to *amortize* the debt on her house over a thirty-year period. This way the monthly payments would be within her budget.
   Definitions will vary.
   _____
   _____

Words

- **amortize**
- **immortalize**
- **morbid**
- **mordant**
- **moribund**
- **mortgage**
- **mortify**
- **mortuary**
- **postmortem**
- **remorse**

4. At his trial the accused admitted his guilt and shed tears of *remorse* for the suffering he had caused his victims.

Definitions will vary.

5. As September turned to October, the vines on my *moribund* tomato plants turned color and began to droop to the ground.

Definitions will vary.

6. Our new stadium was named in honor of our retired principal. The school board felt it was an appropriate way to *immortalize* his efforts to raise money for this important addition to our campus.

Definitions will vary.

7. Because of the mysterious circumstances surrounding the death, the authorities asked for a *postmortem* examination of the body.

Definitions will vary.

8. No one thought that Pablo's *mordant* comments about Bev's pimples were very funny. Why would he want to hurt her so?

Definitions will vary.

9. If you think it is cool to drink and drive, visit the bodies in the *mortuary*. It is full of some very "cool" people who thought the same way.

Definitions will vary.

10. Rolanda was quite *mortified* when Sam was caught stealing copies of the exam. After all, he had been an honors student for two years.

Definitions will vary.

Applying Meaning

Read each sentence or short passage below. Write "correct" on the answer line if the vocabulary word has been used correctly. Write "incorrect" on the answer line if the vocabulary word has been used incorrectly.

1. The committee decorated the dance floor with colorful balloons, put a noisemaker on every table, and hired a lively musical group. This year they wanted a *morbid* atmosphere for the prom.

2. The charge for my surgery was too much to pay all at once. Fortunately, the hospital agreed to *amortize* the debt over a five-year period.

3. It took three days to restore electricity after the storm. By that time most of the food in the refrigerator was too *mortified* to be eaten.

4. After decades of pollution by factories, the lake's *moribund* condition would not be easy to reverse.

5. Before the bank would lend us the money for the business, we had to obtain a *mortgage* on our home.

6. Nadine is one of the most popular people in school. Her broad smile and *mordant* remarks always put everyone in a good mood.

1. __incorrect__

2. __correct__

3. __incorrect__

4. __correct__

5. __correct__

6. __incorrect__

For each word used incorrectly, write a sentence using the word properly.

Answers will vary.

_____

_____

_____

_____

_____

_____

_____

_____

_____

Follow the directions below to write a sentence using a vocabulary word.

7. Write an inscription for a monument or similar memorial. Use any form of the word *immortalize*.

Sample Answer: May this monument immortalize the

memory of our sons and daughters who died in Vietnam.

_____

8. Tell about something that someone you know wishes he or she had not done. Use any form of the word *remorse*.

Sample Answer: Evelyn knew it was wrong to engage in such vicious gossip, but it was too late to stop the rumors now, no matter how much remorse she felt.

9. Write a sentence that might appear in a murder mystery. Use the word *postmortem*.

Sample Answer: The detective could not be sure if the victim had been murdered until the postmortem examination was completed.

10. Complete the following sentence: The medical students visited the *mortuary* in order to . . .

Sample Answer: . . . examine the dead bodies for signs of disease.

Bonus Word

post-

The prefix *post-* comes from the Latin word *post*, meaning "behind" or "after." In English this prefix is used with words or roots to add this Latin meaning, as is the case with *postmortem*.

Build Your Vocabulary: Use the *post-* prefix to write words with the following meanings:

to date something (a check, for example) later than the actual date

postdate

studies taken up after graduation

postgraduate

games played after the season is over

postseason

occurring after one's death (Hint: The prefix combines with a root from the Latin word *humare*, meaning "to bury." The prefix is pronounced differently in this word.)

posthumous

How well do you remember the words you studied in Lessons 22 through 24? Take the following test covering the words from the last three lessons.

Choose the Correct Meaning

Each question below includes a word in capital letters, followed by four words or phrases. Choose the word or phrase that is <u>closest</u> in meaning to the word in capital letters. Write the letter for your answer on the line provided.

Sample

S. FINISH	(A) enjoy	(B) complete	S. ___**B**___
	(C) destroy	(D) send	

1. MORBID	(A) unhappy	(B) filled completely	1. ___**D**___
	(C) calm	(D) unhealthy	
2. INUNDATE	(A) imitate	(B) mark permanently	2. ___**C**___
	(C) flood	(D) undated	
3. AVARICE	(A) greed	(B) good advice	3. ___**A**___
	(C) generosity	(D) patience	
4. INCHOATE	(A) physically weak	(B) in an early stage	4. ___**B**___
	(C) easily digested	(D) interesting	
5. POSTMORTEM	(A) sturdy	(B) shocking	5. ___**D**___
	(C) delayed	(D) done after death	
6. INTEMPERATE	(A) temporary	(B) excessive	6. ___**B**___
	(C) calm and relaxed	(D) greatly reduced	
7. IMMORTALIZE	(A) make unforgettable	(B) protect	7. ___**A**___
	(C) cut in equal parts	(D) push under	
8. STEADFAST	(A) without nourishment	(B) unable to be replaced	8. ___**C**___
	(C) loyal and steady	(D) doubtful	
9. MORDANT	(A) bitingly painful	(B) ignorant	9. ___**A**___
	(C) morally corrupt	(D) magical	
10. VARIABLE	(A) listless	(B) concealed	10. ___**C**___
	(C) changeable	(D) admirable	
11. VIE	(A) deceive	(B) observe from a distance	11. ___**D**___
	(C) secretly destroy	(D) compete for superiority	

Go on to next page. ➤

12. MORTIFY	(A) set in concrete	(B) cause shock or humiliation	12. _____ B
	(C) use as security for a loan	(D) commit a serious sin	
13. RAPACITY	(A) willingness to take by force	(B) remarkable speed	13. _____ A
	(C) mischievous rascal	(D) desire to learn	
14. OBSESS	(A) reverse the direction	(B) preoccupy one's mind	14. _____ B
	(C) infect	(D) injure wrongfully	
15. MORIBUND	(A) delicious	(B) memorable	15. _____ D
	(C) plentiful	(D) near death	
16. REPLETE	(A) repeated regularly	(B) overflowing	16. _____ B
	(C) lacking	(D) dangerous	
17. PROFLIGATE	(A) wasteful	(B) profitable	17. _____ A
	(C) wealthy	(D) insecure	
18. MORTUARY	(A) type of sculpture	(B) place to keep dead bodies	18. _____ B
	(C) moneylender	(D) monument	
19. UNWARY	(A) unused	(B) straight	19. _____ D
	(C) inspired	(D) careless	
20. INDELIBLE	(A) unproven	(B) easily bent	20. _____ C
	(C) permanent	(D) unintentional	
21. REMORSE	(A) sorrow	(B) serious crime	21. _____ A
	(C) joy	(D) doubt	
22. AMORTIZE	(A) destroy	(B) deceive	22. _____ C
	(C) pay a debt in installments	(D) purify with heat	
23. PLUMB	(A) drain	(B) examine closely	23. _____ B
	(C) throw into place	(D) type of fruit	
24. PRISTINE	(A) prison system	(B) pure	24. _____ B
	(C) private	(D) corrupt	
25. PARSIMONY	(A) religious belief	(B) marriage	25. _____ C
	(C) stinginess	(D) official residence	

Name _____

Swamp Features and Creatures

Swamps, marshes, and bogs live in legend as dark, damp, and mysterious places. Many a fictitious monster got its start in the ooze of a swamp on a dark, misty night. In reality, swamps can be **intimidating** places. They often house creatures that sting, bite, and, in extreme circumstances, kill.

5   Swamps, or wetlands as they are currently called, have been a source of interest for centuries. One of the first recorded public works projects was the draining of the Pontine Marshes near Rome, nearly two thousand years ago. The Pontine Marshes were a **notorious** breeding ground for insects, and the Roman authorities wanted to remove this source of danger.

10 Seventeen hundred years later, this **predilection** to eliminate wetlands continued in the newly created United States Congress. Those who **advocated** such a policy convinced Congress to give 64 million acres of federal swampland to the states on the condition that the swamps be drained. One of George Washington's early jobs was to survey the Dismal Swamp in Virginia so it could
15 be drained.

Now scientists have begun to reexamine the role of swamps and the **obsolete** policies of the past. Recent research shows that marshes and swamps play a vital part in **perpetuating** a healthy ecosystem. For example, the coastal marshes along our shores help to purify water before it enters the water table.
20 In addition, these marshes absorb pollutants from water as it flows to the sea. But you don't have to live near a coast to enjoy the benefits of a swamp.

Read any of Mark Twain's stories of life during the **heyday** of the Mississippi River and you get a feel for what the river used to be like. Stretching back from the banks were huge swamps. When the river flooded, these swamps absorbed
25 much of the extra water. Then people started to drain the swamps and build embankments to hold back the river. This allowed farmers and developers to uncover rich, **arable** land and create space to build new **edifices** for growing cities. But although the embankments prevented many smaller floods, the bigger floods overwhelmed the feeble earthen embankments.

30 Specialized swamps called bogs harbor some of the most interesting plants in North America. Situated on acid-tainted water, bogs are usually covered by a floating mat of moss. But more interesting are the unique plants that live on the surface of a bog. Three of these — the pitcher plant, sundew, and Venus's-flytrap — get essential **nutriments** by eating insects. The most interesting
35 method is employed by the Venus's-flytrap. When an insect is attracted to one of the V-shaped leaves, it brushes against triggerlike hairs, causing the leaf to clamp shut and trap the bug. After the insect is digested, the leaf reopens to await its next victim.

As the modern science of ecology begins to shed new light on swamps, a new
40 respect for their value to the environment is developing.

Words
advocate
arable
edifice
heyday
intimidate
notorious
nutriment
obsolete
perpetuate
predilection

Each word in this lesson's word list appears in dark type in the selection you just read. Think about how the vocabulary word is used in the selection, then write the letter for the best answer to each question.

1. In line 3, the word *intimidating* means ____.
   (A) friendly   (B) encouraging
   (C) inspiring   (D) frightening

   1. _____ **D** _____

2. In line 8, the word *notorious* means ____.
   (A) valued for their   (B) respected
       medical uses
   (C) disguised or hidden   (D) well-known for unfavorable reasons

   2. _____ **D** _____

3. In line 10, the word *predilection* means ____.
   (A) opposition   (B) preference
   (C) dislike   (D) lack of interest

   3. _____ **B** _____

4. Which word could best replace *advocated* in line 11?
   (A) opposed   (B) ridiculed
   (C) supported   (D) attacked

   4. _____ **C** _____

5. In line 16, *obsolete* means ____.
   (A) outdated; old   (B) scientifically proven
   (C) expensive   (D) successful

   5. _____ **A** _____

6. Which word could best replace *perpetuating* in line 18?
   (A) eliminating   (B) destroying
   (C) preserving   (D) forgetting

   6. _____ **C** _____

7. In line 22, *heyday* means ____.
   (A) dry season   (B) period of greatest popularity
   (C) harvest season   (D) valley

   7. _____ **B** _____

8. Which word could best replace *arable* in line 27?
   (A) farmable   (B) unproductive
   (C) desert   (D) useless

   8. _____ **A** _____

9. Which word or words could best replace *edifices* in line 27?
   (A) things to eat   (B) buildings
   (C) farmlands   (D) lakes

   9. _____ **B** _____

10. Which word could best replace *nutriments* in line 34?
    (A) nourishments   (B) poisons
    (C) seeds   (D) rocks

    10. _____ **A** _____

Applying Meaning

Follow the directions below to write a sentence using a vocabulary word.

1. Describe something you no longer use. Use any form of the word *obsolete*.

   Sample Answer: After I bought a word processor, my typewriter became obsolete and unusable for most jobs.

2. Tell about something you believe in strongly. Use any form of the word *advocate* in your answer.

   Sample Answer: My advocacy of disarmament is part of a commitment I made to peace in the world.

3. Think of a piece of land you have seen and tell about it. Use the word *arable* in your sentence.

   Sample Answer: The Iowa prairies contain some of the most arable land in the world.

4. Describe the skyline of a city. Use any form of the word *edifice* in your answer.

   Sample Answer: The Sears Tower is the tallest edifice I have ever seen.

5. Describe a person from United States history. Use any form of the word *notorious*.

   Sample Answer: Benedict Arnold is the most notorious traitor in United States history.

6. Describe any method of transportation, past or present. Use the word *heyday*.

   Sample Answer: The heyday of the train occurred between 1860 and 1950.

7. Describe someone, using any form of the word *intimidate*.

Sample Answer: I am always intimidated by the stern look and crossed arms of Principal Schultz.

8. Tell about a favorite food. Use any form of the word *predilection*.

Sample Answer: I have a predilection for deep-fried foods even though they are not good for my health.

Read each sentence below. Write "correct" on the answer line if the vocabulary word has been used correctly. Write "incorrect" on the answer line if the vocabulary word has been used incorrectly.

9. The United States is one of the world's leading *advocates* of democracy.

9. ___correct___

10. Mike is so *arable* the coach rarely lets him play.

10. ___incorrect___

11. The car eventually broke down because nobody ever changed its *nutriments*.

11. ___incorrect___

12. I refused to discuss what I had heard because I did not want to be accused of *perpetuating* rumors.

12. ___correct___

For each word used incorrectly, write a sentence using the word properly.

Answers will vary.

_____

_____

_____

_____

_____

_____

_____

_____

Mastering Meaning

Pick a feature of the landscape in your community. It can be a natural feature of the earth or something that was built. Write a short position paper proposing that this feature be preserved in its present state, destroyed or dismantled, or changed in some way. Use some of the words you studied in this lesson.

Name _____

Open the newspaper or turn on the news, and you will surely see and hear about decline and destruction. People have found many ways to harm and destroy themselves and the things around them. Also, Mother Nature contributes to the devastation with earthquakes, hurricanes, tornadoes, and other natural disasters. In this lesson, you will learn ten words associated with decline and destruction.

Unlocking Meaning

Read the short passages below. Write the letter for the correct definition of the italicized vocabulary word.

As the plane flew over the marshy land, it released a cloud of deadly insecticide. The health department hoped to *decimate* the mosquito population and reduce the risk of disease.

1. (A) identify the location of
   (B) move to another area
   (C) increase the size of
   (D) destroy a large part of

The pool's pumping system removes dirt and other particles from the water. It also keeps the water in the pool moving so that the water does not *stagnate* and become foul.

2. (A) remain motionless
   (B) evaporate too rapidly
   (C) separate
   (D) detach from its surroundings

Your speech is informative and interesting; however, some people in the audience may be offended by that last remark. Since it's not essential to your main idea, I would *expunge* it.

3. (A) memorize
   (B) emphasize
   (C) erase
   (D) intentionally insult

The French Revolution proved to be a *cataclysm* for aristocrats. Some lost their lives; others were forced to flee the country, leaving behind all they owned.

4. (A) violent upheaval
   (B) temporary and annoying inconvenience
   (C) royal pardon
   (D) profitable event

Words
cataclysm
decadence
decimate
depredate
expunge
interpolate
obliterate
putrefaction
stagnate
wane

1. **D**

2. **A**

3. **C**

4. **A**

When the agent from the humane society opened the door, she was almost overcome by the smell of rotting flesh. The animals had been dead for days, and *putrefaction* was well under way.

5. (A) reconstruction
   (B) burial
   (C) legal process
   (D) decay of organic matter

5. _____ **D** _____

Without the leadership of responsible officers, the soldiers began to *depredate* the villagers. By the time they finished, all articles of value had been taken from the town.

6. (A) take charge of
   (B) interrogate
   (C) rob by force
   (D) cause confusion

6. _____ **C** _____

After Tom stormed around the office for five minutes, his anger began to *wane*. A few minutes later, he was his usual calm self.

7. (A) get worse; increase
   (B) become amusing
   (C) become uncontrollable
   (D) lessen; decrease

7. _____ **D** _____

You will confuse your readers if you *interpolate* that paragraph into the con-clusion. I suggest you leave it out.

8. (A) remove
   (B) insert
   (C) eliminate
   (D) divide

8. _____ **B** _____

Winning the lottery eventually led Frieda to live a life of *decadence*. She used to be one of the best students at the academy. Now she spends her time eating, drinking, and gambling.

9. (A) improved sense of values
   (B) decline in morals
   (C) wealth and prosperity
   (D) poverty

9. _____ **B** _____

By setting fire to the house, the criminal hoped to *obliterate* all signs of the theft. The police would assume the missing items were destroyed in the fire.

10. (A) leave behind
    (B) advertise
    (C) eliminate completely
    (D) change the form of

10. _____ **C** _____

Applying Meaning

Read each sentence or short passage below. Write "correct" on the answer line if the vocabulary word has been used correctly. Write "incorrect" on the answer line if the vocabulary word has been used incorrectly.

1. Fierce hurricane winds battered the coast all night and into the morning. Around noon, the winds began to *wane* as the hurricane moved out to sea.

    1.   **correct** _____

2. Since the two businesspeople did not speak the same language, someone was called in to *interpolate* for them.

    2.   **incorrect** _____

3. Carrie says she reads constantly to keep her brain from *stagnating*.

    3.   **correct** _____

4. As editor of the school paper, Serena must read each article and *expunge* any facts that cannot be verified.

    4.   **correct** _____

5. The doctor assured Ms. Morales that it wasn't unusual for a child to suffer from *decadence* after the loss of a grandparent.

    5.   **incorrect** _____

6. After the town's water supply was contaminated by the chemicals, residents were told to *putrefy* all drinking water.

    6.   **incorrect** _____

7. The president said he would not allow the spirit of the country to *depredate* because of the pessimistic attitudes of a few.

    7.   **incorrect** _____

8. The once beautiful landscape was completely *obliterated.* No wildlife could be seen and only a few sickly bushes could grow in the ravaged soil.

    8.   **correct** _____

9. After the *cataclysmic* earthquake of 1994, a number of families decided to move out of California.

    9.   **correct** _____

10. The mayor said he felt honored to be asked to *decimate* the memorial to the heroic police officer.

    10.   **incorrect** _____

For each word used incorrectly, write a sentence using the word properly.

Answers will vary.

_____

_____

_____

_____

_____

_____

_____

_____

_____

_____

_____

_____

_____

_____

Decide which word in parentheses best completes the sentence. Then write the sentence, adding the missing word.

11. A group of parents picketed the adult movie theater and demanded that such ____ establishments be shut down. (decadent; obliterate)

decadent _____

_____

_____

12. By the end of World War II, Berlin had been _____ by continual bombing. (decimated; depredated)

decimated _____

_____

_____

13. Because the boy was only twelve years old at the time of his crime, the judge agreed to _____ his conviction from the records. (expunge; interpolate)

expunge _____

_____

_____

Our Living Language

decimate

In the days of the Roman empire, the punishment for a rebellion in a Roman military unit was the execution of every tenth person in the unit. The term *decimare*, which meant to punish or kill every tenth person, was derived from the Latin word *decem*, meaning "ten." The ranks of such a rebellious faction were thus decimated. Now, of course, *decimate* is used to refer to any large-scale destruction or killing.

Write a Paragraph: Research a historical event in which people were decimated, either by war, disease, or some natural disaster. Explain what happened and tell why you feel the term *decimate* is appropriately applied to this event. Use some of the words you studied in this lesson.

Name _____

A number of English words contain a root taken from the Latin word *carnem,* meaning "flesh." It is easy to see because it almost always appears as *-carn-* in English words and usually keeps some of the original Latin meaning. The Latin word *videre,* meaning "to see," however, may take more than one form in English, such as *-vid-, -vis-,* and *-voy-.* It is a root you need to recognize because it appears in so many English words.

Root	Meaning	English Word
-carn-	flesh	carnivore
-vid-	see	providence
-vis-		visage
-voy-		clairvoyant

Words

- carnage
- carnal
- carnivore
- clairvoyant
- improvise
- incarnate
- invidious
- providence
- reincarnation
- visage

Unlocking Meaning

Write the vocabulary word that fits each clue below. Then say the word and write a short definition. Compare your definition and pronunciation with those given on the flash card.

1. An herbivore feeds on plants; this word is the opposite.

   carnivore. Definitions will vary. _____

   _____

   _____

2. After death, only these fleshy remains are left in the world.

   carnal. Definitions will vary. _____

   _____

   _____

3. This word combines the "see" root with the French word *clair,* meaning "clear." People sometimes consult one to help them find missing persons or things.

   clairvoyant. Definitions will vary. _____

   _____

   _____

4. Everyone has one of these. You can see your own in a mirror.

   visage. Definitions will vary. _____

   _____

   _____

5. This word begins with the prefix *in-* and could be used to complete the sentence, "Some feel that Adolf Hitler was evil . . . ."

incarnate. Definitions will vary.

6. This noun might be applied to a disaster where there was so much bloodshed that flesh was piled upon flesh.

carnage. Definitions will vary.

7. This adjective came into English through the Latin *invidere,* meaning "to look at with envy." It can describe a remark or a look.

invidious. Definitions will vary.

8. In this word the Latin prefix *pro-,* meaning "forward," combines with the "see" root. It can mean "the care and protection of God or nature." When it refers to God, it is capitalized.

providence. Definitions will vary.

9. This word begins with the *re-* prefix, meaning "again." It could be applied to a kind of recycling process.

reincarnation. Definitions will vary.

10. This word begins with a form of the *in-* prefix and literally means "unable to see ahead." If you could not see ahead of time that you were going to be asked to give a speech, you might stand up and do this.

improvise. Definitions will vary.

Applying Meaning

Each question below contains a vocabulary word from this lesson. Answer each question "yes" or "no" in the space provided.

1. At a banquet honoring a foreign guest, would it be appropriate to ask someone to introduce him with a few *invidious* remarks?

2. Would someone move to an isolated cave in a faraway place to get away from the *carnal* temptations of modern civilization?

3. Would you buy carrots, lettuce, and cereal for a *carnivorous* pet?

4. Is it often possible to determine someone's state of mind by studying his or her *visage*?

5. Would the words to an *improvised* song be written down beforehand?

6. Could recycled newspaper be *reincarnated* as a greeting card?

1. ____**no**____
2. ____**yes**____
3. ____**no**____
4. ____**yes**____
5. ____**no**____
6. ____**yes**____

For each question you answered "no," write a sentence using the vocabulary word correctly.

Answers will vary.

_____

_____

_____

_____

_____

_____

_____

_____

_____

_____

_____

Decide which word in parentheses best completes the sentence. Then write the sentence, adding the missing word.

7. The general wanted to avoid the ____ that would result from a prolonged battle, so he proposed a truce to discuss a peace treaty. (carnage; providence)

carnage

_____

_____

8. None of us believed that Madame Zeno possessed _____ powers, but when she predicted an earthquake we could not help being a little frightened. (carnal; clairvoyant)

clairvoyant

_____

_____

9. The principal gives an annual award to the student she feels is the _____ of the values and academic achievements our school tries to represent. (incarnation; visage)

incarnation

_____

_____

10. After repeated rescue attempts failed to reach the stranded hiker, her parents felt there was little to do but to put her fate in the hands of _____. (carnage; Providence)

Providence

_____

_____

Test-Taking Strategies

The Scholastic Aptitude Test (SAT) includes a section on reading comprehension. These tests ask you to read one or two selections and then answer some questions to see how well you understand what you read. The questions do not simply ask you to recall the details—they ask you to draw inferences from the information. For example, if the selection says something about the sound of boots squeaking through snowdrifts, you would be expected to infer that it is winter.

Practice: Reread the selection *Playing Your Cards Right* on page 99. Write an X next to the statements that might be inferred from this essay.

1. Elvis Presley and Buddy Holly were popular in the 1950s.   1. _____ **X** _____

2. Collecting baseball cards is an easy way to make money.   2. _____

3. Before throwing out any baseball cards, you would be wise to see if they are worth money.   3. _____ **X** _____

4. Collecting baseball cards in the 1950s was more popular with boys than with girls.   4. _____ **X** _____

Name _____

25–27

How well do you remember the words you studied in Lessons 25 through 27? Take the following test covering the words from the last three lessons.

Part 1 Choose the Correct Meaning

Each question below includes a word in capital letters, followed by four words or phrases. Choose the word or phrase that is <u>closest</u> in meaning to the word in capital letters. Write the letter for your answer on the line provided.

Sample

S. FINISH	(A) complete	(B) enjoy	**S.**	**A**
	(C) destroy	(D) enlarge		

1. ADVOCATE	(A) annoy	(B) empty	1.	**C**
	(C) promote	(D) warn		
2. INVIDIOUS	(A) disagreeable	(B) transparent	2.	**A**
	(C) charming	(D) amazing		
3. STAGNATE	(A) accuse	(B) instruct	3.	**D**
	(C) praise	(D) become motionless		
4. CATACLYSM	(A) loud noises	(B) catastrophe	4.	**B**
	(C) animal sanctuary	(D) steep cliff		
5. INTIMIDATE	(A) frighten	(B) suggest	5.	**A**
	(C) become very close with another person	(D) deliver		
6. NUTRIMENT	(A) nourishment	(B) rock formation	6.	**A**
	(C) seed	(D) improvement		
7. NOTORIOUS	(A) saintly	(B) decayed	7.	**C**
	(C) famous for unfavorable reasons	(D) secret		
8. IMPROVISE	(A) improve greatly	(B) move cautiously	8.	**D**
	(C) promise	(D) perform without preparation		
9. HEYDAY	(A) period of greatest success	(B) harvest time	9.	**A**
	(C) time of pain or disappointment	(D) source of riches		

Go on to next page. ➤

© NTC Publishing Group

Review and Test 125

| 10. EXPUNGE | (A) soak up | (B) erase | 10. _____**B**_____ |
| | (C) release | (D) bounce | |

| 11. PREDILECTION | (A) type of election | (B) rumor | 11. _____**C**_____ |
| | (C) tendency | (D) taste for adventure | |

| 12. WANE | (A) decrease | (B) trick | 12. _____**A**_____ |
| | (C) move without purpose | (D) seek passionately | |

| 13. ARABLE | (A) likely to make mistakes | (B) foreign | 13. _____**D**_____ |
| | (C) open or uncovered | (D) fertile | |

| 14. PROVIDENCE | (A) divine control | (B) storage area for food | 14. _____**A**_____ |
| | (C) area of land | (D) lengthy explanation | |

| 15. VISAGE | (A) home for a religious person | (B) facial expression | 15. _____**B**_____ |
| | (C) invitation | (D) official visit | |

Part 2 Matching Words and Meanings

Match the definition in Column B with the word in Column A.
Write the letter of the correct definition on the line provided.

Column A	**Column B**

16. edifice   a. dead and decaying organic material   16. _____d_____

17. carnage   b. insert in text   17. _____h_____

18. obliterate   c. meat eater   18. _____e_____

19. perpetuate   d. building   19. _____g_____

20. putrefaction   e. erase without a trace   20. _____a_____

21. decimate   f. embodied in human form   21. _____j_____

22. depredate   g. cause to continue   22. _____i_____

23. carnivore   h. corpses   23. _____c_____

24. interpolate   i. ransack or rob   24. _____b_____

25. incarnate   j. kill or destroy large numbers   25. _____f_____

Name _____

The Art of Horace Pippin

During the 1930s, it was unlikely that a middle-aged African American from a small town in Pennsylvania would achieve success as a painter. Add to this the fact that the man had never studied art, had earned his living as a hotel porter and used-clothes peddler, and had all but lost the use of
5   his right arm. Horace Pippin had one of the most **implausible** careers in the history of twentieth-century art.

Born into a family just one generation removed from slavery, Pippin joined the army in 1917 at the age of twenty-nine. While fighting with the celebrated 369th Colored Infantry Regiment in France, he was shot by a
10   sniper. As therapy for his injured arm, he started decorating discarded cigar boxes, whittling picture frames, and burning images on wood panels with a hot poker. It wasn't until 1930 that he tried oil painting for the first time, propping up his right arm with his left hand.

The subject of Horace Pippin's earliest paintings is World War I. The
15   somber palette and emphasis on weapons and **confrontation** suggest that he was summarizing his response to the devastation of modern warfare rather than evoking specific memories of combat. What is most interesting about these early efforts is the three-dimensional effect of hundreds of layers of paint. Although Pippin subsequently abandoned such heavy
20   layering, he continued to rely on **scrupulously** textured pigment, especially for foliage, textiles, and atmospheric effects.

Pippin's representations of African American life are considered to be the **apogee** of his achievements as a painter who was attentive to popular culture. **Culling** images from magazines, films, and illustrated calendars, he
25   committed **vignettes** of family life and seasonal activities to wood panels from doors, tables, or furniture cases. Often the varnish on the original surface provided the principal coloring. A humble charm **suffuses** these memorable scenes, alive with detail down to each lacy edge of a doily and every braid of a rag rug.

30   In 1937, Horace Pippin's paintings came to the attention of an art critic, who encouraged him to contribute several works to an art show outside of Philadelphia. His paintings were so well received that he was asked to participate in the Museum of Modern Art's traveling exhibition of so-called naive, or **primitive**, art. For a time, Pippin was more famous than Grandma
35   Moses, with tributes from coast to coast and works reproduced in all the major magazines. Unfortunately, his fame was **transient**. He died in 1946, having completed 140 paintings, drawings, and wood panels. In his short but extraordinary career, this self-taught painter **exalted** the commonplace and commemorated his unique vision of history, nature, and people.

Words
apogee
confrontation
cull
exalt
implausible
primitive
scrupulous
suffuse
transient
vignette

Context Clues: Reading in the Humanities

Unlocking Meaning

Each word in this lesson's word list appears in dark type in the selection you just read. Think about how the vocabulary word is used in the selection, then write the letter for the best answer to each question.

1. Which word or words could best replace *implausible* in line 5?   1. ____B____
   (A) not noticeable   (B) difficult to believe
   (C) unwise   (D) irritating

2. A *confrontation* (line 15) can best be described as a(n) _____.   2. ____C____
   (A) moral obligation   (B) amendment to a contract
   (C) conflict   (D) hopeless maneuver

3. Which word or words could best replace *scrupulously* in line 20?   3. ____A____
   (A) conscientiously and   (B) dutifully
       exactly
   (C) temporarily   (D) physically

4. An *apogee* (line 23) can best be described as a(n)_____.   4. ____C____
   (A) unrealistic expectation (B) crucial circumstance
   (C) high point   (D) lifelike portrayal

5. Which word could best replace *culling* in line 24?   5. ____A____
   (A) selecting   (B) discarding
   (C) building   (D) ignoring

6. A *vignette* (line 25) can best be described as a(n) _____.   6. ____D____
   (A) insult   (B) alternative to painting
   (C) formal portrait   (D) short scene or incident

7. Which word or words could best replace *suffuses* in line 27?   7. ____C____
   (A) ruins   (B) reverses
   (C) spreads through   (D) reduces in intensity

8. Which word or words could best replace *primitive* in line 34?   8. ____C____
   (A) happening regularly (B) suitable
   (C) simple and   (D) complex and sophisticated
       unsophisticated

9. Something that is *transient* (line 36) can best be described as _____.   9. ____B____
   (A) extraordinary   (B) of brief duration
   (C) intensely felt   (D) unexpected

10. Which word or words could best replace *exalted* in line 38?   10. ____A____
   (A) elevated   (B) substituted
   (C) developed gradually (D) concealed

Applying Meaning

Follow the directions below to write a sentence using a vocabulary word.

1. Explain the accomplishments of a famous athlete, musician, or politician. Use the word *apogee*.

   Sample Answer: At the apogee of his baseball career,

   Ty Cobb held the world record for runs batted in and

   stolen bases.

2. Describe an example of an art form, hobby, or craft. Use any form of the word *primitive*.

   Sample Answer: Part of the reason for the primitive

   character of early colonial portraits is the fact that artists

   simply filled in the heads on already painted bodies.

3. Describe someone's appreciation of a garden during a particular time of the year. Use any form of the word *transient*.

   Sample Answer: Sandra was relieved to see the crocuses

   poke their heads through melting snow, because she knew

   that their transience would soon give way to summer.

4. Explain one step of a complex or exacting process. Use any form of the word *scrupulous*.

   Sample Answer: Alex taped a section of his design to the

   piece of textured glass, then scrupulously traced its out-

   line before making his first cut.

5. Describe a speech or a speaker you have heard recently. Use any form of the word *exalt*.

   Sample Answer: In their eulogies for the president, the

   speakers exalted his political accomplishments and

   minimized the scandals.

Each question below contains a vocabulary word from this lesson. Answer each question "yes" or "no" in the space provided.

6. Before making a pie, do you *cull* only the sweetest and plumpest blueberries from those you have picked?

   6. _____ **yes**

7. Is a *vignette* a delicate vine that grows in tropical climates?

   7. _____ **no**

8. When people blush, can they sometimes feel the heat and redness *suffuse* their face?

8. _____**yes**_____

9. Is it *implausible* to think an honors student will get a good grade in this class?

9. _____**no**_____

10. Is a *confrontation* a favorable opinion of a person's abilities?

10. _____**no**_____

For each question you answered "no," write a sentence using the vocabulary word correctly.

Answers will vary.

_____

_____

_____

_____

_____

_____

_____

_____

_____

_____

_____

_____

_____

_____

_____

Mastering Meaning

Choose a painter whom you would like to know more about, such as Joan Miró, Salvador Dali, or Grandma Moses. Do some research in the library about this person. Then write a brief biographical sketch, highlighting his or her special achievements. Use some of the words we studied in this lesson.

Name _____

Nothing, it seems, remains the same for long. An ugly caterpillar changes into a beautiful butterfly. A young boy's voice changes pitch as he grows. Styles of clothing change. Political opinions change. One day you are convinced you are right about something; the next day you change your mind. In this lesson, you will learn ten words that relate to change.

Unlocking Meaning

A vocabulary word appears in italics in each sentence or short passage below. Think about how the word is used in the passage. Then write a definition for the vocabulary word. Compare your definition with the definition on the flash card.

Words
capricious
desultory
ephemeral
immutable
inveterate
malleable
metamorphosis
modulate
vacillate
volatile

1. During his entire campaign, the candidate *vacillated* on the issue of taxes. By election day, voters had no idea if he supported or opposed raising taxes.

    Definitions will vary. _____

    _____

    _____

2. That man, an *inveterate* thief, has gone to jail several times for robbery. No amount of punishment seems to be enough to reform him.

    Definitions will vary. _____

    _____

    _____

3. Marta's *desultory* conversation left me totally confused. She never stayed on one subject long enough for me to figure out what she was talking about.

    Definitions will vary. _____

    _____

    _____

4. "When you give a speech," Ms. Arnetto instructed, "*modulate* your voice. Changing from soft tones to louder tones will add expression and maintain the audience's interest."

    Definitions will vary. _____

    _____

    _____

5. The town council's decision to fire the police chief remained *immutable*. The fact that numerous citizens had signed a petition protesting the action would not change the council's decision.

Definitions will vary.

_____

_____

_____

6. In Robert Louis Stevenson's *The Strange Case of Dr. Jekyll and Mr. Hyde,* Dr. Jekyll undergoes a complete *metamorphosis* when he drinks a solution made in his laboratory. The kindly Dr. Jekyll becomes the vicious and cruel Mr. Hyde.

Definitions will vary.

_____

_____

_____

7. A successful company cannot afford to have *capricious* leadership. It is better to set a goal and stick with it than to change directions with each new impulse.

Definitions will vary.

_____

_____

_____

8. Most investors prefer a steady, predictable economy rather than a *volatile* one in which wages and prices go up and down suddenly.

Definitions will vary.

_____

_____

_____

9. Gold is a soft, *malleable* metal that can be hammered and molded into many different shapes. If it were not, there would be very limited amounts of gold jewelry.

Definitions will vary.

_____

_____

_____

10. The rainbow was remarkably beautiful, but its beauty was *ephemeral*. After a few short minutes, its brilliant colors had faded away.

Definitions will vary.

_____

_____

_____

Applying Meaning

Each question below contains a vocabulary word from this lesson. Answer each question "yes" or "no" in the space provided.

1. Would you trust an *inveterate* liar if he told you important news?

2. Would an *ephemeral* thought be on your mind for days and weeks at a time?

3. Would you avoid using a *vacillating* umpire in an important baseball game?

4. Is the law of gravity considered *immutable*?

5. Would a *capricious* person tend to analyze a problem in great detail before acting?

6. Is someone with a *malleable* personality probably easy to get along with?

7. When entering a library or viewing a solemn ceremony, are you expected to *modulate* the volume of your conversation?

8. Is it difficult to take notes on a *desultory* lecture?

9. Could you count on a person with a *volatile* temper to be in a good mood on a given day?

10. Does a tadpole that changes into a frog experience *metamorphosis*?

1. _____ **no** _____
2. _____ **no** _____
3. _____ **yes** _____
4. _____ **yes** _____
5. _____ **no** _____
6. _____ **yes** _____
7. _____ **yes** _____
8. _____ **yes** _____
9. _____ **no** _____
10. _____ **yes** _____

For each question you answered "no," write a sentence using the vocabulary word correctly.

Answers will vary.

_____
_____
_____
_____
_____
_____
_____
_____
_____
_____
_____
_____

Follow the directions below to write a sentence using a vocabulary word.

11. Describe something you or someone you know did. Use the word *capricious*.

Sample Answer: Being in a capricious frame of mind, Jasper suddenly put down his hammer, picked up his fishing rod, and left for the lake.

12. Use the word *volatile* to describe something.

Sample Answer: When Mr. Higgin's volatile temper suddenly erupted, the meeting turned into a shouting match.

13. Use *inveterate* to describe a personality trait of someone you know.

Sample Answer: An inveterate optimist, Coach Madison insisted that her team could overcome the opponent's twenty-point lead and win the game.

14. Describe a sound you commonly hear. Use any form of the word *modulate*.

Sample Answer: The modulating sounds of the sirens warned motorists of the rapidly approaching emergency vehicles.

	Bonus Word
●	**chameleon**
	A *chameleon* is a type of lizard that lives in the forests of Africa, Madagascar, Asia, and Spain. The most remarkable feature of these short, flat, slow-moving reptiles is their ability to change color. When frightened or exposed to a variation in temperature or light, a chameleon may change from green to black, from yellow to brown, from a solid color to spots. A person who changes opinions, attitudes, and behavior to suit his or her surroundings is often described as a *chameleon*.
	Cooperative Learning: Work with a partner to brainstorm a list of animals whose names might be used to describe human traits or personalities. Create an "Animal Adjective Dictionary." For each dictionary entry, write the animal's name and its most remarkable features, and explain how it is used to describe people.

Name _____

The Latin root *-pel-* is seen in many familiar words. It comes from the Latin word *pellere*, meaning "to drive" or "to push." This root also appears in English words as *-puls-*. You probably know many words that contain the root *-vit-* or *-viv-*. This root comes from the Latin word *vivere*, meaning "to live." Each vocabulary word in this lesson has one of these two roots.

Root	Meaning	English Word
-pel-	to drive, to push	impel
-puls-		pulsate
-vit-	to live	vitality
-viv-		vivacious

Words

compulsory

convivial

dispel

impel

pulsate

repellent

viable

victual

vitality

vivacious

Unlocking Meaning

Write the vocabulary word that fits each clue below. Then say the word and write a short definition. Compare your definition and pronunciation with those given on the flash card.

1. This verb begins with a form of the prefix *in-*, meaning "against." It literally means "drive against."

   impel. Definitions will vary. _____

   _____

   _____

2. This word is an adjective that ends in a suffix meaning "capable of." You see the French word *vie*, meaning "life," in this word.

   viable. Definitions will vary. _____

   _____

   _____

3. This word is always a verb. A healthy heart will "drive" like this regularly.

   pulsate. Definitions will vary. _____

   _____

   _____

4. This adjective might be used to describe someone with a charming and witty personality or who seems to be full of life.

   vivacious. Definitions will vary. _____

   _____

   _____

5. This adjective begins with the prefix *com-*, meaning "with," and contains a form of the "push" root. When a meeting is this, you *have* to be there.

compulsory. Definitions will vary.

6. This word has a prefix meaning "away" and may be an adjective or a noun. It comes in handy around mosquitoes because it drives them away.

repellent. Definitions will vary.

7. This word is always a noun. You do not have this if you are tired and sluggish.

vitality. Definitions will vary.

8. This adjective also begins with a prefix that means "with." You might use this word to describe someone who enjoys lively parties with lots of people.

convivial. Definitions will vary.

9. This verb is a combination of the "drive" root and the *dis-* prefix, meaning "apart."

dispel. Definitions will vary.

10. It is not easy to see the "live" meaning in this word until you realize that life depends on food. It has three vowels, but its pronunciation has only two syllables.

victual. Definitions will vary.

Applying Meaning

Follow the directions below to write a sentence using a vocabulary word.

1. Describe an elderly person or someone famous. Use the word *vitality*.

   Sample Answer: Although my great-grandfather is eighty-two, he has the vitality of someone half his age.

   _____

2. Use any form of the word *dispel* in a sentence about a false rumor.

   Sample Answer: I was quick to dispel the rumor that Jason had been hurt in a car crash since I knew he was home with the flu.

3. Describe being near a swamp or state an idea you dislike very much. Use the word *repellent*.

   Sample Answer: Because of the mosquitoes, you might want to apply insect repellent before going for a walk around the swamp.

4. Describe a street scene. Use any form of the word *pulsate*.

   Sample Answer: The crowded street pulsated with the life and energy of the city.

   _____

5. Describe a classmate's or a celebrity's personality. Use the word *vivacious*.

   Sample Answer: Katrina's vivacious spirit is contagious, making everyone around her feel energized and lively.

   _____

6. Write a sentence about camping. Use any form of the word *victual*.

   Sample Answer: The cooking equipment was stored in a tent, but the victuals were kept in a tree to prevent bears from getting at them.

7. Write a sentence about the effects of a guilty conscience. Use any form of the word *impel*.

Sample Answer: Her guilty conscience impelled her to come forward and tell the truth about the broken window.

Decide which word in parentheses best completes the sentence. Then write the sentence, adding the missing word.

8. After hours of discussion, Jorge's proposal still seemed like the most _____ plan. (convivial; viable)

viable

9. Before being hired as a truck driver, each applicant had to pass a _____ drug test. (compulsory; vivacious)

compulsory

10. A _____ mood was in evidence when the meeting began, but as soon as the subject of declining sales came up, things changed rapidly. (convivial; compulsory)

convivial

	Bonus Word
⬤	**joie de vivre**
	A hearty, carefree person who seems to love and enjoy every moment of his or her life may be said to have *joie de vivre* (zhwä′ də vē′vrə). This familiar expression, which has worked its way into the English language from French, translates as "joy of living."
	Write a Paragraph: Do you know anyone with true *joie de vivre*? Perhaps that someone is you. Write a paragraph describing a person with *joie de vivre*, providing details of how the person's joy of living is demonstrated.

How well do you remember the words you studied in Lessons 28 through 30? Take the following test covering the words from the last three lessons.

Part 1 Antonyms

Each question below includes a word in capital letters, followed by four words or phrases. Choose the word or phrase that is most nearly <u>opposite</u> in meaning to the word in capital letters. Consider all choices before deciding on your answer. Write the letter for your answer on the line provided.

Sample

| S. HIGH | (A) cold | (B) simple | S. ___C___ |
| | (C) low | (D) foolish | |

| 1. COMPULSORY | (A) required | (B) optional | 1. ___B___ |
| | (C) sudden | (D) simple | |

| 2. CAPRICIOUS | (A) clumsy | (B) unconnected | 2. ___D___ |
| | (C) stale | (D) constant | |

| 3. IMPLAUSIBLE | (A) unlikely | (B) probable | 3. ___B___ |
| | (C) without pauses | (D) attractive | |

| 4. MALLEABLE | (A) rigid | (B) portable | 4. ___A___ |
| | (C) impossible | (D) counterfeit | |

| 5. VACILLATE | (A) awaken | (B) deny | 5. ___C___ |
| | (C) remain unchanged | (D) lubricate | |

| 6. VIABLE | (A) invisible | (B) genuine | 6. ___C___ |
| | (C) unable to survive | (D) solid | |

| 7. REPELLENT | (A) attractive | (B) repeated often | 7. ___A___ |
| | (C) calm | (D) sickly appearance | |

| 8. IMMUTABLE | (A) loud | (B) easily changed | 8. ___B___ |
| | (C) lovable | (D) attractive | |

| 9. SCRUPULOUS | (A) humorous | (B) illogical | 9. ___D___ |
| | (C) honest | (D) careless | |

| 10. DESULTORY | (A) well organized | (B) complimentary | 10. ___A___ |
| | (C) pure | (D) harmful | |

Go on to next page. ➤

11. MODULATE   (A) simplify   (B) proceed without change   11. ___**B**___

     (C) modify   (D) examine closely

12. EPHEMERAL   (A) essential   (B) plain   12. ___**C**___

     (C) long-lived   (D) commonplace

13. PRIMITIVE   (A) complex   (B) related to animals   13. ___**A**___

     (C) artistic   (D) dangerous

14. INVETERATE   (A) experienced   (B) changeable   14. ___**B**___

     (C) confusing   (D) tending to arouse anger

15. VIVACIOUS   (A) deceitful   (B) possessing high moral principles   15. ___**D**___

     (C) easily embarrassed   (D) dull

Part 2 Matching Words and Meanings

Match the definition in Column B with the word in Column A.
Write the letter of the correct definition on the line provided.

Column A	Column B		
16. apogee	a. conflict	16.	f
17. volatile	b. drive away	17.	h
18. dispel	c. select	18.	b
19. cull	d. force into action	19.	c
20. confrontation	e. jovial	20.	a
21. pulsate	f. highest or farthest point	21.	j
22. victual	g. food	22.	g
23. convivial	h. explosive	23.	e
24. impel	i. spread through	24.	d
25. suffuse	j. throb	25.	i

Name _____

Salvaging History: The Wreck of the Ten Sail

Somewhere, far below the deceptively **placid** turquoise waters off the Cayman Islands, lies an important piece of history. Although the wrecks of the British frigate HMS *Convert* and nine of its fifty-eight-ship merchant convoy will never **relinquish** the treasures of Spanish galleons, they may
5   provide historians with the opportunity to reconstruct part of eighteenth-century maritime life and culture.

The position of the Cayman Islands, along the sailing route of the Leeward Passage, ensured that from the earliest days of New World exploration, seafarers used them as navigational landmarks. Ever since the
10   sixteenth century, the coral reefs surrounding the islands have been a **pernicious** snare for hundreds of ships, including the *Convert.*

A popular version of this shipwreck dates it to 1788 and mentions a naval escort. Other stories suggest that the **calamity** was caused by pirate ships. Although the traditional narratives related in the islands diverge from his-
15   torical fact, the folkloric title "Wreck of the Ten Sail" stuck. During the eighteenth century, "ten sail" referred to ten sailing ships.

Eighteenth-century official documents **procured** from the archives of Great Britain and Jamaica reveal an intriguing story. According to this source, the HMS *Convert* was bound from Jamaica to Great Britain in February 1794,
20   under the command of Captain John Lawford. With the frigate as a **bulwark**, the convoy of merchant vessels were **laden** with West Indian sugar and rum. At the beginning of the journey, the fleet was delayed by a leaky merchant ship, preventing the *Convert's* officers from sighting Grand Cayman before sunset on the second day of the voyage. At midnight, the sailing master rec-
25   ommended to the captain that their course be shifted more to the north, in order to reach the western tip of Cuba. By his reckoning, the fleet was south-west of Grand Cayman. A few hours later, however, several ships that had sailed ahead wrecked on the reefs of the largest island. One of these ships fired a warning shot, and the captain of the *Convert* gave the signal for the
30   convoy to **disperse**. As the frigate attempted to change course, a merchant vessel crashed into her bow and became entangled. By the time the *Convert* cleared the other ship, she was too near the breakers to escape. The dawn revealed nine merchant vessels and their naval escort hopelessly aground on the reef. At least eight people perished in the disaster.

35   The crew **salvaged** some of the cargo from the ships involved in the "Wreck of the Ten Sail" before they sank. The specific location of the debris was forgotten, and for two centuries, the sites were taken over by the sea. Today, there are plans to recover **relics**, such as cannons, anchors, ships' fittings, and navigational instruments. Underwater archaeologists antic-
40   ipate contributing to Caymanian as well as maritime history.

Words
bulwark
calamity
disperse
laden
pernicious
placid
procure
relic
relinquish
salvage

Unlocking Meaning

Each word in this lesson's word list appears in dark type in the selection you just read. Think about how the vocabulary word is used in the selection, then write the letter for the best answer to each question.

1. In line 1 *placid* means ____.
   - (A) dangerous
   - (B) transparent
   - (C) smelling like fish
   - (D) calm

   1. ____ **D** ____

2. Which word could best replace *relinquish* in line 4?
   - (A) surrender
   - (B) separate
   - (C) authorize
   - (D) locate

   2. ____ **A** ____

3. Which word could best replace *pernicious* in line 11?
   - (A) forceful
   - (B) spirited
   - (C) harmful
   - (D) symbolic

   3. ____ **C** ____

4. A *calamity* (line 13) can best be described as a(n) ____.
   - (A) disaster
   - (B) exchange of views
   - (C) strange situation
   - (D) series of steps

   4. ____ **A** ____

5. Something that is *procured* (line 17) can best be explained as ____.
   - (A) obtained by special effort
   - (B) released to the public
   - (C) taken illegally
   - (D) translated

   5. ____ **A** ____

6. Which word or words could best replace *bulwark* in line 20?
   - (A) incentive
   - (B) decoy
   - (C) example
   - (D) defense or safeguard

   6. ____ **D** ____

7. Which word or words could best replace *laden* in line 21?
   - (A) influenced by tides
   - (B) unrestrained
   - (C) weighed down by
   - (D) incapable of being subdued

   7. ____ **C** ____

8. Which words could best replace *disperse* in line 30?
   - (A) return to port
   - (B) scatter in different directions
   - (C) examine the damage
   - (D) identify the problem

   8. ____ **B** ____

9. Something that is *salvaged* (line 35) can best be described as ____.
   - (A) saved from loss
   - (B) thrown about
   - (C) turned in a circular motion
   - (D) ruined

   9. ____ **A** ____

10. *Relics* (line 38) can best be described as ____.
    - (A) vulnerable targets
    - (B) different combinations of parts
    - (C) historically interesting objects
    - (D) minor weaknesses

    10. ____ **C** ____

Name _____

Applying Meaning

Decide which word in parentheses best completes the sentence. Then write the sentence, adding the missing word.

1. On April 15, 1912, the ocean liner *Titanic* sank in what is considered one of the greatest _____ in maritime history. (calamities; relics)

   calamities _____

   _____

   _____

2. When its ships were repeatedly harassed by German submarines, the United States _____ its neutrality and entered World War I on the side of Great Britain, France, Russia, and Italy. (procured; relinquished)

   relinquished _____

   _____

   _____

3. The system of checks and balances was designed as a _____ against the accumulation of too much power by one branch of the government. (bulwark; dispersal)

   bulwark _____

   _____

   _____

4. During the 1920s, the discovery of Tutankhamen's unplundered tomb was among the great archaeological discoveries of the time; well-preserved _____ provided scientists with information about life in Egypt and the pharaoh's reign. (relics; bulwarks)

   relics _____

   _____

   _____

5. Oona's decisiveness and her _____ temperament make her the perfect candidate for the position of sales manager in the department store's bargain basement. (placid; pernicious)

   placid _____

   _____

   _____

Read each sentence below. Write "correct" on the answer line if the vocabulary word has been used correctly. Write "incorrect" on the answer line if the vocabulary word has been used incorrectly.

6. *Laden* with backpacks, tents, cooking equipment, and a four-day supply of food, the donkey plodded slowly up the trail.

6.   **correct**

7. The committee chairperson *dispersed* with the reading of the minutes from the last meeting because of the lateness of the hour.

7.   **incorrect**

8. When it discovers *pernicious* medical treatments or devices through testing, the FDA approves these new methods and products to improve life and health.

8.   **incorrect**

9. Many of the hurricane victims were unable to *salvage* even a single possession; strong winds and water had destroyed everything.

9.   **correct**

10. The Erie Canal was an important factor in encouraging immigration to the Midwest, helping to *procure* numerous large cities.

10.   **incorrect**

For each word used incorrectly, write a sentence using the word properly.

Answers will vary.

_____

_____

_____

_____

_____

_____

_____

_____

_____

_____

_____

Mastering Meaning

In spite of the best intentions, not everything we plan turns out exactly as we expected. Forces like nature or other people are often beyond our control. Write a serious or humorous narrative about a situation that got out of hand. Be sure to explain the original plan as well as how the outcome deviated from it. Use some of the words you studied in this lesson.

Name _____

Life is made up of a number of starts and stops. Every day is a series of new starts at school, on the job, or at play. We begin new friendships, learn new skills, and travel new roads. At the same time we bring things to a close. We leave behind old friends, move on to new jobs, and find new interests. The words in this lesson are related to the many ways we start, stop, or pause to think things over.

Unlocking Meaning

Read the sentences or short passages below. Write the letter for the correct definition of the italicized vocabulary word.

We were certain that the icy roads would *impede* our travel, so we left for the airport an hour early.

1. (A) hasten
    (B) hinder
    (C) ignore
    (D) enhance

Megan knew she had to finish her homework before class met on Monday, but as usual she had *procrastinated.* Once again she was doing her homework at midnight on Sunday.

2. (A) prepared carefully
    (B) offended others
    (C) finished quickly
    (D) postponed until later

For the two hours that the storm raged, we took shelter in the basement. When the wind and rain finally began to *abate*, we were able to go outside and survey the damage.

3. (A) lessen
    (B) increase
    (C) move unpredictably
    (D) turn to the west

The Petersens decided to place their pets in a kennel while they were on vacation. Since many hotels and parks do not allow pets, the Petersens did not wish to *fetter* themselves by bringing the animals.

4. (A) expand
    (B) shorten
    (C) restrict one's freedom
    (D) explain

Words
abate
debut
encumber
fetter
impede
inhibit
neophyte
precipitate
procrastinate
thwart

1. ____**B**____

2. ____**D**____

3. ____**A**____

4. ____**C**____

The automobile manufacturer refused to allow the reporters to photograph the new solar-powered car. If photographs appeared in the newspapers now, the car's *debut* at the energy conference would be spoiled.

5. (A) first public appearance
   (B) destruction
   (C) competition
   (D) remodeling

5. _____A_____

Because Maria was a *neophyte*, she paid too much for the stamps. An experienced collector would have bargained for a better price.

6. (A) well-known expert
   (B) native
   (C) beginner
   (D) someone unable to make a decision

6. _____C_____

Even though the two nations were discussing a peace treaty, the hostile behavior of the border guards was certain to *precipitate* a war.

7. (A) prevent
   (B) postpone indefinitely
   (C) make impossible
   (D) cause to happen

7. _____D_____

The cold, rainy weather *inhibited* the repair work on the cottage. The project will now take two more months to complete.

8. (A) held back
   (B) improved slightly
   (C) destroyed
   (D) moved from place to place

8. _____A_____

Thinking the rescuers were going to harm his master, the growling dog *thwarted* all efforts to treat the injured hiker.

9. (A) improved
   (B) prevented
   (C) admired
   (D) ignored

9. _____B_____

The retreating soldiers left behind their heavy weapons. In order to make a quick retreat, they could not be *encumbered* by unnecessary weight.

10. (A) burdened
    (B) moved to action
    (C) joined together
    (D) deceived

10. _____A_____

Name _____

Applying Meaning

Each question below contains a vocabulary word from this lesson. Answer each question "yes" or "no" in the space provided.

1. Would a convicted murderer be *fettered* while being tranported to prison?

2. Would someone who constantly *procrastinates* make a good emergency medical technician?

3. If you needed surgery for a serious injury, would you request that a *neophyte* perform the operation?

4. After a field trip to the theater, might your teacher ask the class to write a *debut* of the play?

5. Could forecasts of an approaching hurricane *precipitate* a traffic jam on the freeways leading out of town?

6. Would having your leg in a cast be an *encumbrance* when climbing a steep flight of stairs?

1. _____ **yes**

2. _____ **no**

3. _____ **no**

4. _____ **no**

5. _____ **yes**

6. _____ **yes**

For each question you answered "no," write a sentence using the vocabulary word correctly.

Answers will vary.

_____

_____

_____

_____

_____

_____

_____

_____

_____

Follow the directions below to write a sentence using a vocabulary word.

7. Tell about a time you or someone you know controlled a feeling of anger. Use any form of the word *abate*.

Sample Answer: I allowed my anger to abate before I

calmly asked my neighbor to remove his dog from my

garden.

8. Describe a time when you were very frustrated by something. Use any form of the word *thwart*.

Sample Answer: The sound from my brother's television continued to thwart my efforts to take a nap.

9. Describe something that interfered with someone's plans or activities. Use any form of the word *inhibit*.

Sample Answer: The injuries our quarterback suffered in practice inhibited his movements during the game.

10. Describe a project or similar activity that took longer than you planned. Use any form of the word *impede*.

Sample Answer: The loss of my notes seriously impeded my work on the research paper and caused me to turn it in three days late.

Our Living Language

The word *neophyte* came into English through the Greek *neo-* meaning "new" and *phytos* meaning "planted." A neophyte is "newly planted" in some field and therefore is a beginner. The Greek word part *neo-* is frequently added to the beginning of a word to add the meaning of "new" or "different" to another word. It is usually used to refer to a rebirth or revitalization of a previous concept or idea. Hence, a movement to reintroduce the beliefs or methods of Hitler's fascism might be referred to as *neofascism* or *neo-Nazism*.

Build Your Vocabulary: Add the Greek *neo-* to these words to make a new word. Then use a dictionary to write a brief definition for each word.

| Darwinism | expressionism | Freudian |
| colonialism | liberal | classicism |

The Roots -polis-, -polit-, and -urb-

Name _____

Two closely related Greek words show up in many English words. The first, *polites*, is the Greek word for "citizen," and can be found in words like *politic*. The second, *polis*, means "city." It is seen in the English word *megalopolis*. In Latin the root for "city" is *-urb-*. It is found in English words like *urban*. All the words in this lesson contain one of these roots.

Root	Meaning	English Word
-polit-	citizen	politic
-polis-	city	megalopolis
-urb-	city	urban

Words

- **cosmopolitan**
- **geopolitics**
- **impolitic**
- **megalopolis**
- **metropolitan**
- **politic**
- **politico**
- **urban**
- **urbane**
- **urbanite**

Unlocking Meaning

Write the vocabulary word that fits each clue below. Then say the word and write a short definition. Compare your definition and pronunciation with those given on the flash card.

1. This word is a combination of the Greek word *megas*, meaning "great," and the Greek word for "city." An example would be the cluster of large cities near New York City in northern New Jersey.

   megalopolis. Definitions will vary.
   _____
   _____

2. This adjective comes from the Greek word for "citizen" and describes a type of behavior. Some say it is the type of behavior a successful politician would probably have.

   politic. Definitions will vary.
   _____
   _____

3. Originating with the Greek word for "citizen," this English word has come to refer to a citizen involved in government. Perhaps because the word came into English through Italian, a final *o* was added.

   politico. Definitions will vary.
   _____
   _____

4. This noun combines "politics" and "geography." It suggests that how nations view each other depends on a combination of these.
   geopolitics. Definitions will vary.

5. This adjective comes from the Greek *metropolis*, meaning "mother city." It is often used to describe a city and its outlying areas, or two large, closely connected cities, like Dallas–Fort Worth and Minneapolis–Saint Paul.
   metropolitan. Definitions will vary.

6. From the Latin word for "city," this adjective is the opposite of "rural."
   urban. Definitions will vary.

7. This adjective also comes from the Latin word for "city," but it describes a manner or behavior. It is probably based on the belief that people living in cities have better manners.
   urbane. Definitions will vary.

8. This adjective is a combination of the Greek *kosmos*, meaning "world" or "universe," and the Greek word for "citizen."
   cosmopolitan. Definitions will vary.

9. This word ends with the suffix *-ite*, meaning "a person of or from."
   urbanite. Definitions will vary.

10. This word adds a form of the *in-* prefix, meaning "not," to the root meaning "citizen." It has more to do with politics than with citizenship.
    impolitic. Definitions will vary.

Applying Meaning

Each question below contains at least one vocabulary word from this lesson. Answer each question "yes" or "no" in the space provided.

1. Would you expect an *urbane* man or woman to behave properly in a social gathering?

2. Would you be likely to find an *urbanite* living in a *megalopolis*?

3. If someone you just met made an *impolitic* remark, would he or she make a good first impression?

4. In planning a subway linking a city and all of its surrounding areas, would it be sensible to consult representatives from the *metropolitan* area?

5. Would a *cosmopolitan* man or woman be interested only in hometown issues and events?

6. Would an *urban* setting include dirt roads, and small, wooden cabins?

1. ___**yes**___

2. ___**yes**___

3. ___**no**___

4. ___**yes**___

5. ___**no**___

6. ___**no**___

For each question you answered "no," write a sentence using the vocabulary word(s) correctly.

Answers will vary.

_____

_____

_____

_____

_____

_____

_____

_____

_____

Follow the directions below to write a sentence using a vocabulary word.

7. Describe a remark or comment someone made while running for office. Use the word *politic*.

Sample Answer: Senator Birdwell made the rather politic

remark that she was not going to make her opponent's

arrest for reckless driving a campaign issue.

8. Use any form of the term *geopolitics* in a sentence about an international problem or issue.

Sample Answer: A number of geopolitical factors were given as reasons for not sending United States ground troops into the troubled nation.

9. Choose a well-known *politico* involved in local, state, or federal government. Then complete this sentence: Like most politicos, (your chosen example) always . . . .

Sample Answer: Like most politicos, Matt Rudford always manages to get his picture in the newspapers whenever the government is building a new bridge.

10. Write a sentence describing what you might expect to see in a megalopolis. Use the word *megalopolis* in your sentence.

Sample Answer: The megalopolis was crowded with people, buses, and cars moving slowly through the streets.

Bonus Word

Spartan

Sparta was the capital of the ancient Greek city-state of Laconia. Ruled by a small group of people whose ancestors had conquered the area around 1100 B.C., Sparta expected the male members of the ruling class to survive on the barest essentials and to endure the most brutal hardships. Today, if someone leads a Spartan existence, he or she leads a life of frugality and strict self-discipline.

Cooperative Learning: The names of certain cities and states are sometimes used today to refer to the lifestyles of the people who live there. What does it mean to have a California look? How long is a New York minute? Work with a partner to list some terms and definitions that are based on a city or state.

Name ____________________

How well do you remember the words you studied in Lessons 31 through 33? Take the following test covering the words from the last three lessons.

Part 1 Choose the Correct Meaning

Each question below includes a word in capital letters, followed by four words or phrases. Choose the word or phrase that is closest in meaning to the word in capital letters. Write the letter for your answer on the line provided.

Sample

S. FINISH	(A) enjoy (C) destroy	(B) complete (D) enlarge	**S.** B
1. URBANE	(A) crowded (C) refined	(B) proud (D) talkative	**1.** C
2. ABATE	(A) lessen (C) desire	(B) argue (D) tempt	**2.** A
3. FETTER	(A) humiliate (C) accelerate	(B) restrain (D) decide quickly	**3.** B
4. PLACID	(A) attractive (C) peaceful	(B) soft (D) unusual	**4.** C
5. SALVAGE	(A) uncivilized (C) guard closely	(B) save (D) frighten	**5.** B
6. IMPOLITIC	(A) illegal (C) forceful	(B) impolite (D) unwise	**6.** D
7. COSMOPOLITAN	(A) handsome (C) worldly	(B) foreign (D) crude	**7.** C
8. NEOPHYTE	(A) beginner (C) habitual thief	(B) elected official (D) coward	**8.** A
9. PERNICIOUS	(A) suspicious (C) improper	(B) destructive (D) amusing	**9.** B
10. MEGALOPOLIS	(A) early form of life (C) large monument	(B) harsh noises (D) large populated area	**10.** D

Go on to next page. ➤

11. BULWARK   (A) wide street   (B) safeguard   11.   **B**
        (C) threat   (D) idle conversation

12. PROCRASTINATE   (A) postpone   (B) support strongly   12.   **A**
        (C) mislead   (D) brush aside

13. DEBUT   (A) argument   (B) denial   13.   **D**
        (C) explanation   (D) first appearance

14. IMPEDE   (A) move aside   (B) gain speed   14.   **C**
        (C) hinder   (D) trick

15. CALAMITY   (A) false claim   (B) disaster   15.   **B**
        (C) unit of measure   (D) misunderstanding

Part 2 Matching Words and Meanings

Match the definition in Column B with the word in Column A.
Write the letter of the correct definition on the line provided.

Column A	Column B		
16. relic	a. politician	16.	b
17. metropolitan	b. remains from the past	17.	f
18. urbanite	c. get through effort	18.	j
19. procure	d. cause to occur	19.	c
20. inhibit	e. give up	20.	h
21. disperse	f. having to do with a city	21.	i
22. relinquish	g. loaded	22.	e
23. precipitate	h. restrain	23.	d
24. politico	i. scatter	24.	a
25. laden	j. person who lives in a city	25.	g

Name _____

The Most Important Chemical Reaction in the World

After the cold gray of winter, spring brings a sense of freshness and renewal. The **salutary** effect of the new season has been celebrated in festivals and ceremonies for centuries. Perhaps more than anything else, the green sprouts that burst from the soil and gradually **elongate** upward reflect this annual
5 renewal. After witnessing this **phenomenon** year after year, one might begin to take this rebirth of plant life for granted. In reality, however, it is quite amazing. A little sunny warmth, some water, soil, and seeds can **endow** a field with explosions of flowers and a dense green cover in just a few weeks. How can a field that was frozen in lifeless ice and snow in February produce such
10 **grandeur** in April and May? How can an orchard that was bleak and bare in March produce bushels of fruit in September? And how does the harvest of this growth sustain almost all other life on earth year around?

These questions address the very core of life itself. Almost all life on earth is powered by energy **imparted** by the sun. Living things that make their
15 own food, such as plants, are called autotrophs. These autotrophs capture energy from the sun and use it directly or store it for future use. Other organisms, called heterotrophs, eat autotrophs and extract the energy and nutrients stored in their cells. Thus, directly or indirectly, the energy that powers almost all life is **derived** from the sun. But what allows plants
20 to change sunlight into the stuff of life?

Within the cells of plants are chemicals that cause reactions to take place. In this case, the key chemical is chlorophyll. It is critical to the most important chemical reaction in the living world—photosynthesis. During this seemingly simple reaction, solar energy and chlorophyll cause the carbon diox-
25 ide and water in the atmosphere to combine and form sugar and oxygen.

But the reaction is not really as simple as it seems, for there are a number of steps. First a series of steps called the light reactions bind the energy of light into molecules that are later used to build sugar molecules. The solar energy is absorbed by chlorophyll and converted into chemical energy
30 stored in the bonds of an intermediate compound. During this phase, water is **decomposed**, ultimately giving off oxygen and leaving hydrogen ions behind. This oxygen is then **accessible** to you and other living things.

Other steps in this process of photosynthesis do not require light energy and are therefore called the dark reactions. During this stage the energy
35 from the intermediate chemical, the hydrogen ions, and carbon dioxide combine into simple sugars. These simple sugars and the atoms they contain are the building blocks from which almost all other living tissue is built.

Photosynthesis is the **pivotal** chemical reaction of human existence. So long as we have it, we have the means to survive.

Words

accessible

decompose

derive

elongate

endow

grandeur

impart

phenomenon

pivotal

salutary

Unlocking Meaning

Each word in this lesson's word list appears in dark type in the selection you just read. Think about how the vocabulary word is used in the selection, then write the letter for the best answer to each question.

1. Which word could best replace *salutary* in line 2?
   (A) demoralizing   (B) confusing
   (C) religious   (D) beneficial

   1. _____D_____

2. Which word could best replace *elongate* in line 4?
   (A) lengthen   (B) shorten
   (C) retract   (D) demand

   2. _____A_____

3. A *phenomenon* (line 5) is a _____.
   (A) noteworthy event (B) game
   (C) photograph   (D) serious crisis

   3. _____A_____

4. In line 7, *endow* means _____.
   (A) take away   (B) supply
   (C) discard   (D) subtract

   4. _____B_____

5. In line 10, the word *grandeur* means _____.
   (A) ugliness   (B) magnificence
   (C) confusion   (D) tallness

   5. _____B_____

6. Which word or words could best replace *imparted* in line 14?
   (A) given   (B) removed
   (C) taken away   (D) concealed

   6. _____A_____

7. Which word could best replace *derived* in line 19?
   (A) predicted   (B) ignored
   (C) hidden   (D) received

   7. _____D_____

8. Which word or words could best replace *decomposed* in line 31?
   (A) built   (B) written down
   (C) broken down   (D) assembled

   8. _____C_____

9. Which word could best replace *accessible* in line 32?
   (A) explained   (B) available
   (C) denied   (D) unpleasant

   9. _____B_____

10. In line 38, the word *pivotal* means_____.
    (A) extremely important (B) unnecessary
    (C) sensible   (D) repulsive

    10. _____A_____

Applying Meaning

Follow the directions below to write a sentence using a vocabulary word.

1. Describe a place or building in your community. Use any form of the word *accessible* in your description.

   Sample Answer: Goodfellow Park is not accessible from

   Belcher Street.

   _____

2. Describe what happens to a garden at the end of the growing season. Use any form of the word *decompose* in your answer.

   Sample Answer: As the weather turned cold, the

   withered tomato vines began to decompose.

   _____

3. Think of something that gives you or someone you know great pleasure. State this in a sentence using any form of the word *derive*.

   Sample Answer: June derives great pleasure from

   collecting the signatures of her favorite baseball players.

   _____

4. Tell about waiting in line for an event. Use any form of the word *elongate* in your answer.

   Sample Answer: We were lucky to get to the basket-

   ball game early, since the ticket line became elongated

   shortly after we arrived.

5. Describe something valuable you learned or received from an important person in your life. Use any form of the word *endow*.

   Sample Answer: My mother endowed me with an appre-

   ciation for the importance of getting a good education.

   _____

6. Tell about a beautiful scene you have seen in person, on television, or in movies. Use the word *grandeur* in your answer.

   Sample Answer: The grandeur of the Sierra Nevada

   mountain range is difficult to capture even in a

   photograph.

Read each sentence below. Write "correct" on the answer line if the vocabulary word has been used correctly. Write "incorrect" on the answer line if the vocabulary word has been used incorrectly.

7. Our principal is very *accessible*; he always keeps his door open for students.

7. ____**correct**____

8. The teacher was delighted that the students had *imparted* the lesson.

8. ____**incorrect**____

9. The astronaut walked to the *pivotal* that had been placed on the stage, unfolded her notes, and began her speech.

9. ____**incorrect**____

10. Since a full solar eclipse is such a rare *phenomenon*, scientists try to observe it closely.

10. ____**correct**____

11. The *salutary* effects of the contaminated water caused the campers to become quite ill.

11. ____**incorrect**____

12. Often the children of well-known athletes are also *endowed* with exceptional physical ability.

12. ____**correct**____

For each word used incorrectly, write a sentence using the word properly.

Answers will vary.

Mastering Meaning

The process of photosynthesis is one of the most important phenomena in nature. Without it, life as we know it on our planet could not exist. Think of another important phenomenon. It does not have to be as critical as photosynthesis, but it should be something you think is important for life as you know it. Describe this phenomenon in a short essay and tell why you think it is important. Use some of the words from this lesson.

Lesson
35
Part A

Name _____

Matters of truth and falsehood are not always simple cases of right and wrong. Our language includes a number of words that allow us to be less blunt or to imply degrees of falsehood. Even truth occurs by degrees. It is not surprising that someone sworn to tell the truth is advised that it must be "the truth, the whole truth, and nothing but the truth." This lesson looks at ten words that deal with the concepts of truth and falsehood.

Unlocking Meaning

Read the short passages below. Write the letter for the correct definition of the italicized vocabulary word.

Words
artifice
beguile
belie
bona fide
chicanery
fabricate
feign
probity
veracity
veritable

Everyone in class smiled broadly when Jack insisted that he had to take care of his sick cat over the weekend and therefore could not finish his homework. Jack had *fabricated* such excuses before, but this was the most ridiculous one we had ever heard.

1. (A) decided against
   (B) made up
   (C) rejected
   (D) enjoyed

Even though Mayor Ramos admitted that her administration had made serious mistakes, she was re-elected by a sizable majority. Voters apparently admired her *veracity* more than they worried about a few honest mistakes.

2. (A) deceptive statement
   (B) political connections
   (C) blunt behavior
   (D) truthfulness

As he approached the foul line, Ezra's calm appearance and confident stride *belied* the nervousness he felt inside. If he missed this basket, the season would be over for the team.

3. (A) contradicted
   (B) revealed
   (C) celebrated
   (D) exaggerated

When Judge Walker learned that she had once met the defendant, she withdrew from the trial. Even though the lawyers were certain she would be fair, Judge Walker's *probity* would not allow even the appearance of bias.

4. (A) integrity; honesty
   (B) meaningless gesture
   (C) clever trick
   (D) illegal activity

1. _____**B**_____

2. _____**D**_____

3. _____**A**_____

4. _____**A**_____

It was just like Victor to come up with some *artifice* for getting out of help-ing us build the float. Not only did the cast on his arm have a zipper, the so-called broken bone healed the next day.

5. (A) genuine problem or concern
   (B) helpful advice
   (C) crafty trick
   (D) emotional speech

5. _____ **C** _____

Before the museum would agree to buy the painting, the dealer had to prove that it was a *bona fide* Rembrandt. Only an expert could distinguish between a true original and a good copy.

6. (A) imitation
   (B) colorful
   (C) inexpensive
   (D) genuine

6. _____ **D** _____

The lecture on South American art was dreadfully boring, but I did not want to insult the speaker. So instead of yawning or staring at the ceiling, I *feigned* interest by appearing to take notes.

7. (A) delayed
   (B) pretended
   (C) refused to accept
   (D) concealed

7. _____ **B** _____

When the star quarterback was injured in the first quarter, losing the game seemed a *veritable* certainty. He had scored all of the points in the last game.

8. (A) joyful
   (B) unusual
   (C) unquestionable
   (D) senseless

8. _____ **C** _____

Do not allow their cute appearance to *beguile* you into thinking they cannot harm you. Lion cubs have sharp claws that can cut very deeply.

9. (A) deceive
   (B) amaze
   (C) enlighten
   (D) warn

9. _____ **A** _____

Just before the starting gun fired, Jason pointed to the sky and yelled, "Look out!" This was not the first time he had used such *chicanery* in an effort to win a blue ribbon.

10. (A) sportsmanship
    (B) heroic effort
    (C) curiosity
    (D) trickery

10. _____ **D** _____

Applying Meaning

Read each sentence or short passage below. Write "correct" on the answer line if the vocabulary word has been used correctly. Write "incorrect" on the answer line if the vocabulary word has been used incorrectly.

1. When visiting Toronto, you must see the SkyDome. It is the most impressive *artifice* I have ever seen.

2. The senator deeply resented the suggestion that she had lied during the campaign. No one had ever questioned her *veracity* before.

3. Before paying thousands of dollars for the desk, the dealer insisted that an expert examine it to determine if it was a *bona fide* antique.

4. The mission was extremely dangerous. Because the *probity* of survival was very small, only volunteers would be asked to undertake it.

5. Some gamblers *beguile* their opponent into thinking they are just learning how to play the game. Then after their opponent makes a large bet, they suddenly become very skillful at the game.

6. The weather in the desert is actually quite *veritable*. Even though the temperature might reach one hundred degrees in the afternoon, the nights can be quite cool.

1. __incorrect__
2. __correct__
3. __correct__
4. __incorrect__
5. __correct__
6. __incorrect__

For each word used incorrectly, write a sentence using the word properly.

Answers will vary.

_____
_____
_____
_____
_____
_____
_____
_____
_____

Decide which word in parentheses best completes the sentence. Then write the sentence, adding the missing word.

7. The police were certain that the suspect's story was a total _____ after he claimed he was at the movies on the night of the crime but could not remember which movie he saw. (fabrication; veracity)

fabrication _____
_____
_____

8. The boy's father never really cared much for baseball, but for the sake of his son, he _____ interest in the sport and went to all the Little League games. (belied; feigned)

feigned _____

_____

_____

9. Before an applicant is accepted into the military academy, the admissions committee must be convinced of his or her _____ . (chicanery; veracity)

veracity _____

_____

_____

10. His rusty old car and faded clothes _____ the fact that he was the wealthy owner of several successful companies. (belied; beguiled)

belied _____

_____

_____

	Bonus Word
●	**candid**
	The ancient Romans had a special word for a particularly pure, almost
	glowing type of white. The verb was *candere*, meaning "to shine." The
	adjective was *candidus*, meaning "pure white." The Latin *candidatus*,
	from which we get *candidate*, meant "clothed in white," from the white
	togas worn by those seeking office. The modern English word *candid*
	also comes from this Latin word. A candid person is one who is open,
	sincere, and honest. The word *candid* also means unrehearsed. A candid
	photograph is one taken without the subject's knowledge.
	Cooperative Learning: A candid remark can be truthful and sincere,
	but it can also be honest to the point of being rude or painful. Complete
	the following statement containing the word *candid:*
	I would never say this to anyone else, but my candid opinion of . . . is . . .

Name _____

The Latin word *gignere* means "to beget" or "to produce." This root appears as -gen- in a number of English words. Another Latin word, *genus*, means "kind," as in "that kind of book." It is related to the Greek word *genos*, meaning "race" or "kind." The root also appears as -gen- in English words.

Root	Meaning	English Word
-gen-	to produce	progeny
-gen-	race, kind	gender

Unlocking Meaning

A vocabulary word appears in italics in each short passage below. Find the root in the vocabulary word and think about how the word is used in the passage. Then write a definition for the vocabulary word. Compare your definition with the definition on the flash card.

1. The activists claimed the billboards caused residential neighborhoods to *degenerate* into unsightly slums.

   Definitions will vary. _____

   _____

   _____

2. Their living room has a *heterogeneous* collection of furniture. One chair is modern. Another is an antique, and the lamp is from the 1950s.

   Definitions will vary. _____

   _____

   _____

3. Felipe and I have a most *congenial* relationship. We both love going to horror movies and spending hours at the library.

   Definitions will vary. _____

   _____

   _____

4. Many of the plots in Shakespeare's plays had their *genesis* in earlier plays or in the stories of the period. This borrowing was not unusual in Elizabethan England because artists valued the classics more than originality.

   Definitions will vary. _____

   _____

   _____

Words
congenial
congenital
degenerate
gender
generic
genesis
genre
heterogeneous
primogeniture
progeny

5. In some societies, the entire community, rather then just the parents, takes responsibility for raising their *progeny*. Under this arrangement, all of the adults share the tasks of teaching and caring for all of the children.

Definitions will vary.

_____

_____

6. A baby whose mother drank heavily during pregnancy is more likely to have a *congenital* birth defect.

Definitions will vary.

_____

_____

7. By today's standards, the medieval law of *primogeniture* seems unfair. In those days, only the first-born male could inherit the family's wealth or title. Nowadays, however, all children usually share in the family's estate.

Definitions will vary.

_____

_____

8. Only since 1970 have newspapers removed *gender* classifications from advertisements for employment. Before that time it was generally agreed that only certain types of jobs were appropriate for women.

Definitions will vary.

_____

_____

9. Thomas Hardy is well known for his novels, but few realize that fiction was not the only *genre* in which he excelled. His poetry is also much admired by the critics.

Definitions will vary.

_____

_____

10. Jess insists on buying the expensive, brand-name orange juice. I think the *generic* type is just as good, and it costs less.

Definitions will vary.

_____

_____

Applying Meaning

Follow the directions below to write a sentence using a vocabulary word.

1. Write a sentence describing a crowd of people. Use the word
heterogeneous in your sentence.

Sample Answer: The rally for the presidential candidate

attracted a heterogeneous crowd from every ethnic, reli-

gious, and geographical element of the city.

2. Tell about something you read recently. Use the word *genre*.

Sample Answer: Although poetry is not my favorite liter-

ary genre, I do enjoy the poems of Elizabeth Bishop.

3. Write a rule for the correct use of the pronoun *he, him, she,* or *her.*
Use the word *gender.*

Sample Answer: If a personal pronoun refers to some-

one of the male gender, use *he* or *him.*

4. Use *progeny* in a sentence about your family or a family you know.

Sample Answer: All ten of the Williamsons' progeny

have graduated from college.

5. Describe an event such as an athletic contest or a debate that turned
into something else. Use any form of the word *degenerate* in your
sentence.

Sample Answer: The debate began as an orderly discus-

sion, but after twenty minutes it degenerated into a

shouting match.

Each question below contains a vocabulary word from this lesson.
Answer each question "yes" or "no" in the space provided.

6. Are highly advertised products often available in *generic* form?

6. ____**yes**____

7. Would you expect good friends to have a *congenital* relationship?

7. ____**no**____

8. Do anthropologists sometimes travel to remote areas to study the
primogeniture that live there?

8. ____**no**____

9. Is it desirable for a sales representative to have a *congenial* association with his or her customers?

__yes__

10. In the famous children's story, does the beautiful swan have its *genesis* as an ugly duckling?

10. __yes__

For each question you answered "no," write a sentence using the vocabulary word correctly.

Answers will vary.

_____

_____

_____

_____

_____

_____

_____

Test-Taking Strategies

Tests are often used to evaluate a student's mastery of standard English grammar and usage. These tests ask you to look at four underlined parts of a sentence and decide if one of the parts contains an error. You are then asked to write the letter for the part containing an error. If there is no error, you write "E."

Always read the entire sentence before deciding on your answer. To test whether you have identified an error, ask yourself how you would correct the error.

Practice: Write the letter for the underlined part of the sentence with an error. If there is no error, write E.

1. Everyone <u>who</u> lives near the bank or works in the area <u>was asked</u>
        A   B
<u>to describe</u> what <u>they</u> saw. <u>No Error</u>
   C   D   E

__D__

2. With <u>it's</u> head resting <u>on the pillow</u>, <u>Butch</u>, <u>our pet spaniel</u>, was the
      A   B   C   D
picture of contentment. <u>No Error</u>
                   E

__A__

3. <u>Anyone</u> expecting to get a <u>passing</u> grade in this course must arrive on
   A   B
time for every class, <u>complete</u> all homework <u>on time</u>, and pass an oral
                    C   D
examination. <u>No Error</u>
          E

__E__

166   The Root -gen-

© NTC Publishing Group

Name _____

How well do you remember the words you studied in Lessons 34 through 36? Take the following test covering the words from the last three lessons.

Part 1 Choose the Correct Meaning

Each question below includes a word in capital letters, followed by four words or phrases. Choose the word or phrase that is <u>closest</u> in meaning to the word in capital letters. Write the letter for your answer on the line provided.

Sample

S. FINISH	(A) enjoy	(B) complete	S.	**B**
	(C) destroy	(D) send		

1. BONA FIDE	(A) well cooked	(B) genuine	1.	**B**
	(C) luxurious	(D) plain		
2. PROGENY	(A) intelligence	(B) tiny organisms	2.	**C**
	(C) children	(D) ancestors		
3. BELIE	(A) misrepresent	(B) surprise	3.	**A**
	(C) encourage	(D) relax		
4. ACCESSIBLE	(A) undeniable	(B) accidental	4.	**C**
	(C) available	(D) highly technical		
5. ELONGATE	(A) press down	(B) delay	5.	**D**
	(C) enclose	(D) lengthen		
6. PIVOTAL	(A) pointed	(B) unusually strong	6.	**D**
	(C) athletic	(D) crucial		
7. GENRE	(A) type	(B) gentleness	7.	**A**
	(C) prediction	(D) argument		
8. CONGENIAL	(A) inherited	(B) hostile	8.	**D**
	(C) controversial	(D) pleasant		
9. FEIGN	(A) offend	(B) pretend	9.	**B**
	(C) explain	(D) capture		
10. HETEROGENEOUS	(A) creative	(B) identical	10.	**C**
	(C) mixed	(D) hesitant		

Go on to next page. ➤

11. IMPART   (A) allow   (B) convey   11. _____**B**_____
                     (C) remove   (D) dismiss

12. SALUTARY   (A) rigid   (B) celebrated   12. _____**C**_____
                     (C) beneficial   (D) unhealthy

13. GENERIC   (A) general   (B) sexual   13. _____**A**_____
                     (C) corrupt   (D) ancient

14. DERIVE   (A) decide   (B) obtain   14. _____**B**_____
                     (C) ridicule   (D) excuse

15. VERACITY   (A) bravery   (B) common sense   15. _____**D**_____
                     (C) false accusation   (D) truthfulness

Part 2 Matching Words and Meanings

Match the definition in Column B with the word in Column A.
Write the letter of the correct definition on the line provided.

Column A	**Column B**	
16. veritable	a. trickery	16. _____c_____
17. chicanery	b. sexual category	17. _____a_____
18. degenerate	c. unquestionable	18. _____i_____
19. genesis	d. deceive	19. _____j_____
20. grandeur	e. provide	20. _____f_____
21. phenomenon	f. splendor	21. _____h_____
22. beguile	g. integrity	22. _____d_____
23. endow	h. event	23. _____e_____
24. gender	i. worsen	24. _____b_____
25. probity	j. origin	25. _____g_____

Lesson 3

gre·gar·i·ous (grĭ-gâr'ē-əs) *adj.* 1. Fond of the company of others; sociable. 2. Living in flocks or groups. **-gre·gar'i·ous·ly,** *adv.* **-gre·gar'i·ous·ness,** *n.*

in·junc·tion (ĭn-jŭngk'shən) *n.* 1. A command; order. 2. A court order requiring or prohibiting some act.

junc·ture (jŭngk'chər) *n.* 1. The act of joining or the state of being joined. 2. A point where two things are joined.

jun·ta (hoŏn'tə, jŭn'-) *n.* A group, usually made up of military officers, that rules a country after the overthrow of the government.

seg·re·gate (sĕg'rĭ-gāt') *v.* **-gat·ed, -gat·ing.** 1. To set apart from others; isolate. 2. To impose the separation of a specific group from the rest of society.

Lesson 3

adjunct (ăj'ŭngkt') *n.* Something added to another thing but not essential to it. *-adj.* Added or connected in a subordinate capacity.

ag·gre·gate (ăg'rĭ-gĭt) *adj.* Gathered together into a whole; total. *-n.* A whole composed of a mass of distinct things. *-v.* To gather into a mass.

con·gre·gate (kŏng'grĭ-gāt') *v.* **-gat·ed, -gat·ing.** To gather into a crowd or mass; assemble. **-con'gre·ga'tion,** *n.*

e·gre·gious (ĭ-grē'jəs, -jē-əs) *adj.* Remarkably bad or offensive; flagrant. **-egre'gious·ly,** *adv.* **-egre'gious·ness,** *n.*

enjoin (ĕn-join') *v.* 1. To direct, order, or urge with authority. 2. To prohibit; forbid. **-enjoin'er,** *n.* **-enjoin'ment,** *n.*

Lesson 2

e·go·cen·tric (ē'gō-sĕn'trĭk, ĕg'ō-) *adj.* Interested only in one's own needs or affairs; self-centered. **-e'go·cen'trically,** *adv.* **-e'go·cen·tric'i·ty,** *n.*

haugh·ty (hô'tē) *adj.* **-ti·er, -ti·est.** Having or showing great pride in oneself and scorn for others. **-haugh'ti·ly,** *adv.* **-haugh'ti·ness,** *n.*

pom·pous (pŏm'pəs) *adj.* Characterized by too much dignity or self-importance. **-pom·pos'i·ty, pom'pous·ness,** *n.* **-pom'pous·ly,** *adv.*

un·pre·ten·tious (ŭn'prĭ-tĕn'shəs) *adj.* Modest; simple; plain. **-un'pre·ten'tious·ly,** *adv.* **-un'pre·ten'tious·ness,** *n.*

wasp·ish (wŏs'pĭsh) *adj.* Easily irritated or annoyed; bad-tempered. **-wasp'ish·ly,** *adv.* **-wasp'ish·ness,** *n.*

Lesson 2

ar·ro·gant (ăr'ə-gənt) *adj.* Feeling or showing an overbearing pride or self-importance; conceited; haughty. **-ar'ro·gance,** *n.*

cav·a·lier (kăv'ə-lîr') *adj.* Showing a haughty or disdainful disregard for; sometimes in a free and easy manner. **-cav'a·lier'ly,** *adv.*

con·de·scend·ing (kŏn'dĭ-sĕn'dĭng) *adj.* Showing a snobbish or superior attitude. **-con'descend'ingly,** *adv.*

con·temp·tu·ous (kən-tĕmp'choō-əs) *adj.* Showing disdain or contempt; scornful. **-con·temp'tu·ous·ly,** *adv.* **-con·temp'tu·ous·ness,** *n.*

e·bul·lient (ĭ-boŏl'yənt, ĭ-bŭl'-) *adj.* 1. Very enthusiastic. 2. Boiling; bubbling. **-ebul'lience, ebul'lien·cy,** *n.* **-ebul'lient·ly,** *adv.*

Lesson 1

keen (kēn) *adj.* 1. Very strong; intense. 2. Having or showing mental quickness. 3. Very sensitive. 4. Piercing; cutting. **-keen'ly,** *adv.*

leg·a·cy (lĕg'ə-sē) *n., pl.* **-cies.** 1. Something handed down from the past as from an ancestor. 2. Money or property left to someone by a will.

nu·ance (noō'äns', nyoō'-, noō-äns', nyoō-) *n.* A slight variation in meaning, expression, color, or tone.

rep·er·toire (rĕp'ər-twär') *n.* A list of artistic works, such as plays, operas, or songs, that a performer or group is prepared to perform.

stark (stärk) *adj.* 1. Utter; complete; absolute. 2. Bleak; desolate; barren. 3. Harsh; grim. **-stark'ly,** *adv.* **-stark'ness,** *n.*

Lesson 1

a·droit (ə-droit') *adj.* Skillful and clever; resourceful. **-adroit'ly,** *adv.* **-adroit'ness,** *n.*

em·body (ĕm-bŏd'ē) *v.* **-bod·ied, -body·ing, -bodies.** 1. To give definite or concrete form to. 2. To incorporate. **-em·bod'i·ment,** *n.*

foi·ble (foi'bəl) *n.* A minor weakness in character.

fu·gi·tive (fyoō'jĭ-tĭv) *adj.* 1. Passing away quickly; not lasting long. 2. Fleeing. *-n.* A person who flees. **-fu'gi·tive·ly,** *adv.* **-fu'gi·tive·ness,** *n.*

ir·re·press·i·ble (ĭr'ĭ-prĕs'ə-bəl) *adj.* Incapable of being restrained or controlled. **-ir're·press'i·bil'i·ty, -ir're·press'i·bly,** *adv.*

Lesson 3 gregarious	Lesson 3 adjunct	Lesson 2 egocentric	Lesson 2 arrogant	Lesson 1 keen
Lesson 3 injunction	Lesson 3 aggregate	Lesson 2 haughty	Lesson 2 cavalier	Lesson 1 legacy
Lesson 3 juncture	Lesson 3 congregate	Lesson 2 pompous	Lesson 2 condescending	Lesson 1 nuance
Lesson 3 junta	Lesson 3 egregious	Lesson 2 unpretentious	Lesson 2 contemptuous	Lesson 1 repertoire
Lesson 3 segregate	Lesson 3 enjoin	Lesson 2 waspish	Lesson 2 ebullient	Lesson 1 stark

Lesson 1 adroit
Lesson 1 embody
Lesson 1 foible
Lesson 1 fugitive
Lesson 1 irrepressible

Lesson 4

ar·cane (är-kān´) *adj.* Known or understood by only those with special knowledge; hidden or secret.

ar·chives (är´kīvs´) *n.* **1.** A place where public records or historical documents are kept. **2.** The records or documents kept there.

cir·cum·scribe (sûr´kəm-skrīb´) *v.* **-scribed, -scrib·ing. 1.** To limit; confine; restrict. **2.** To draw a line around; encircle.

cov·ert (kŭv´ərt, kō´vərt, kō-vûrt´) *adj.* Secret; disguised; hidden; concealed. **-cov´ert·ly,** *adv.* **-cov´ert·ness,** *n.*

dis·patch (dĭ-spăch´) *n.* **1.** A written message sent with speed. **2.** A news story sent by a reporter to a news service. *-v.* To send on specific business.

Lesson 4

fa·cil·i·ty (fə-sĭl´ĭ-tē) *n., pl.* **-ties.** Ease of doing, moving, or acting due to aptitude or skill.

hone (hōn) *v.,* **-honed, -hon·ing. 1.** To sharpen. **2.** To perfect or make more effective. *-n.* A whetstone used to sharpen tools.

in·cred·u·lous (ĭn-krĕj´ə-ləs) *adj.* **1.** Unbelieving; skeptical. **2.** Showing doubt or disbelief. **-in·cred´u·lous·ly,** *adv.* **-in·cred´u·lous·ness,** *n.*

pol·y·glot (pŏl´ē-glŏt´) **1.** Speaking, writing, or understanding several languages. *-n.* A person who speaks, writes, or understands several languages.

sur·mount (sər-mount´) *v.* **1.** To overcome; conquer. **2.** To climb up or over. **-sur·mount´a·ble,** *adj.* **-sur·mount´er,** *n.*

Lesson 5

ap·pease (ə-pēz´) *v.* **-peased, -peas·ing. 1.** To satisfy; relieve. **2.** To pacify by giving in to demands. **3.** To bring peace or calm to.

ar·bi·tra·tion (är´bĭ-trā´shən) *n.* A method of settling a dispute in which an impartial person or group reaches a decision. **ar´bi·trate´,** *v.*

at·ta·ché (ăt´ə-shā´, ă-tā-) *n.* A member of a diplomatic staff, especially in a particular capacity.

con·cil·i·a·to·ry (kən-sĭl´ē-ə-tôr´ē, -tōr´ē) *adj.* Meant to win over or to overcome the hostility of. **-con·cil·i·a´tion,** *n.*

con·su·late (kŏn´sə-lĭt) *n.* The official office or residence of a government representative who resides in a foreign country.

Lesson 5

en·tente (ŏn-tŏnt´) *n.* An understanding or agreement between two or more countries.

pla·cate (plā´kāt´, plăk´āt´) *v.* **-cat·ed, -cat·ing.** To calm the anger of; pacify. **-pla´cat·er,** *n.* **-pla·ca´tion,** *n.*

pro·pi·tious (prə-pĭsh´əs) *adj.* Favorable; opportune; auspicious. **-pro·pi´tious·ly,** *adv.* **-pro·pi´tious·ness,** *n.*

pro·to·col (prō´tə-kôl´, -kōl´, -kŏl´) *n.* The ceremonial customs and rules of polite behavior observed by diplomats and others.

proxy (prŏk´sē) *n., pl.* **-ies. 1.** A person authorized to act for another. **2.** A document authorizing a person to act for another.

Lesson 6

abjure (ăb-jŏŏr´) *v.* **-jured, -jur·ing. 1.** To give up on oath; renounce. **2.** To give up; abstain from. **-ab·jura´tion,** *n.* **-abjur´er,** *n.*

ad·ju·di·cate (ə-jōō´dĭ-kāt´) *v.* **-cat·ed, -cat·ing.** To hear and decide a case by judicial procedure. **-adju·di·ca´tion,** *n.*

con·jure (kŏn´jər, kən-jŏŏr´) *v.* **-jured, -jur·ing. 1.** To bring to mind. **2.** To summon by using magic words.

dem·a·gogue (dĕm´ə-gŏg´, -gôg´) *n.* A leader who gains power by appealing to the emotions and prejudices of the people.

dem·o·graph·ics (dĕm´ə-grăf´ĭks, dē´mə-) *pl. n.* The social characteristics of human populations, such as age, gender, and income.

Lesson 6

en·dem·ic (ĕn-dĕm´ĭk) *adj.* Prevalent in or restricted to a particular place or people. **-en·dem´i·cal·ly,** *adv.*

ju·di·cious (jōō-dĭsh´əs) *adj.* Having or showing sound judgment; wise. **-ju·di´cious·ly,** *adv.* **-ju·di´cious·ness,** *n.*

ju·ris·dic·tion (jŏŏr´ĭs-dĭk´shən) *n.* **1.** The legal right to exercise authority. **2.** Authority. **3.** The territory over which authority is exercised.

ju·ris·pru·dence (jŏŏr´ĭs-prōōd´ns) *n.* **1.** The science or philosophy of law. **2.** A system of laws.

per·jure (pûr´jər) *v.* **-jured, -jur·ing.** To make (oneself) guilty of deliberately telling a lie while under oath. **-per´jur·er,** *n.*

Lesson 6 endemic	Lesson 6 judicious	Lesson 6 jurisdiction	Lesson 6 jurisprudence	Lesson 6 perjure
Lesson 6 abjure	Lesson 6 adjudicate	Lesson 6 conjure	Lesson 6 demagogue	Lesson 6 demographics
Lesson 5 entente	Lesson 5 placate	Lesson 5 propitious	Lesson 5 protocol	Lesson 5 proxy
Lesson 5 appease	Lesson 5 arbitration	Lesson 5 attaché	Lesson 5 conciliatory	Lesson 5 consulate
Lesson 4 facility	Lesson 4 hone	Lesson 4 incredulous	Lesson 4 polyglot	Lesson 4 surmount
Lesson 4 arcane	Lesson 4 archives	Lesson 4 circumscribe	Lesson 4 covert	Lesson 4 dispatch

Lesson 9	Lesson 9	Lesson 9	Lesson 9	Lesson 9
sem·blance (sĕm'bləns) n. 1. Outward appearance. 2. A likeness; copy.	**sim·i·le** (sĭm'ə-lē) n. A figure of speech in which two distinct things are compared by using *like* or *as*.	**sim·u·late** (sĭm'yə-lāt') v. -lat·ed, -lat·ing. 1. To have the appearance, form, or sound of; imitate. 2. To give a false appearance of; pretend.	**tran·spire** (trăn-spīr') v. -spired, -spir·ing. 1. To occur; happen. 2. To become known.	**ver·i·si·mil·i·tude** (vĕr'ə-sĭ-mĭl'ĭ-tood', -tyood') n. The appearance of being true or real.

Lesson 9	Lesson 9	Lesson 9	Lesson 9	Lesson 9
as·pi·rant (ăs'pər-ənt, ə-spīr'-) n. A person who ambitiously seeks something, such as a high position, advancement, or honors.	**as·sim·i·late** (ə-sĭm'ə-lāt') v. -lat·ed, -lat·ing. 1. To absorb and incorporate into oneself. 2. To absorb into a dominant culture.	**en·sem·ble** (ŏn-sŏm'bəl) n. 1. A group of parts producing a single effect. 2. A set of matching clothes. 3. A group of performers.	**ex·pi·ra·tion** (ĕk'spə-rā'shən) n. A coming to an end; termination.	**in·spi·ra·tion** (ĭn'spə-rā'shən) n. 1. Stimulation of the mind, emotions, or imagination. 2. Something that stimulates the mind, emotions, or imagination.

Lesson 8	Lesson 8	Lesson 8	Lesson 8	Lesson 8
in·gen·u·ous (ĭn-jĕn'yoo-əs) adj. 1. Frank and open; straightforward. 2. Innocent; artless; naive. -in·gen'u·ous·ly, adv. -in·gen'u·ous·ness, n.	**per·se·cute** (pûr'sĭ-kyoot') v. -cut·ed, -cut·ing. To subject to cruel, harmful, or unjust treatment, especially because of race, religion, or beliefs.	**pros·e·cute** (prŏs'ĭ-kyoot') v. -cut·ed, -cut·ing. To conduct legal action against.	**pre·cede** (prĭ-sēd') v. -ced·ed, -ced·ing. To be, go, or come before, as in order, rank, importance, or time.	**pro·ceed** (prō-sēd', prə-) v. 1. To go on, especially after stopping. 2. To begin or carry on some action.

Lesson 8	Lesson 8	Lesson 8	Lesson 8	Lesson 8
ad·verse (ăd-vûrs', ăd'vûrs') adj. 1. Unfavorable. 2. Antagonistic; unfriendly. -ad·verse'ly, adv. -ad·verse'ness, n.	**a·verse** (ə-vûrs') adj. Strongly opposed to; unwilling. -a·verse'ly, adv. -a·verse'ness, n.	**floun·der** (floun'dər) v. 1. To move or struggle awkwardly. 2. To speak or act clumsily or in a confused manner.	**foun·der** (foun'dər) v. 1. To fill with water and sink. 2. To fail utterly.	**in·gen·ious** (ĭn-jēn'yəs) adj. 1. Made or done with cleverness and inventiveness. 2. Clever; inventive. -in·gen'ious·ly, adv. -in·gen'ious·ness, n.

Lesson 7	Lesson 7	Lesson 7	Lesson 7	Lesson 7
gos·sa·mer (gŏs'ə-mər) adj. Thin, light, or delicate. -n. 1. A filmy cobweb floating in the air. 2. Something light, delicate, or flimsy.	**ir·i·des·cent** (ĭr'ĭ-dĕs'ənt) adj. Displaying an interplay of rainbowlike colors. -ir'i·des'cence, n. -ir'i·des'cent·ly, adv.	**nox·ious** (nŏk'shəs) adj. Harmful to health or morals; unwholesome. -nox'ious·ly, adv. -nox'ious·ness, n.	**pal·at·a·ble** (păl'ə-tə-bəl) adj. 1. Pleasant to the taste. 2. Pleasing to the mind. -pal'at·a·ble·ness, n. pal'at·a·bil'i·ty, n. pal'at·a·bly, adv.	**tan·dem** (tăn'dəm) adv. One behind the other; in single file. -adj. Working or occurring in conjunction with each other.

Lesson 7	Lesson 7	Lesson 7	Lesson 7	Lesson 7
as·sault (ə-sôlt') n. A violent attack. -v. To attack.	**au·gur** (ô'gər) v. 1. To predict; foretell. 2. To foreshadow; to serve as an omen of. -n. A prophet.	**bev·y** (bĕv'ē) n., pl. -ies. 1. A group. 2. A group of birds or animals, especially quail.	**ca·reen** (kə-rēn') v. 1. To lurch from side to side while in motion. 2. To lean sideways; tilt.	**cui·sine** (kwĭ-zēn') n. 1. The style of preparing food. 2. The food prepared, as at a restaurant.

Lesson 9 verisimilitude	Lesson 9 transpire	Lesson 9 simulate	Lesson 9 simile	Lesson 9 semblance
Lesson 9 inspiration	Lesson 9 expiration	Lesson 9 ensemble	Lesson 9 assimilate	Lesson 9 aspirant
Lesson 8 proceed	Lesson 8 precede	Lesson 8 prosecute	Lesson 8 persecute	Lesson 8 ingenuous
Lesson 8 ingenious	Lesson 8 founder	Lesson 8 flounder	Lesson 8 averse	Lesson 8 adverse
Lesson 7 tandem	Lesson 7 palatable	Lesson 7 noxious	Lesson 7 iridescent	Lesson 7 gossamer
Lesson 7 cuisine	Lesson 7 careen	Lesson 7 bevy	Lesson 7 augur	Lesson 7 assault

Lesson 12	Lesson 12	Lesson 12	Lesson 12	Lesson 12
in·flex·i·ble (ĭn-flĕk′sə-bəl) *adj.* **1.** Not easily bent; stiff; rigid. **2.** Unyielding in mind, principle, or purpose. -**in·flex′i·bil′i·ty**, *n.*	**con·flu·ence** (kŏn′flōō-əns) *n.* **1.** A flowing together of two or more streams. **2.** The place of this. **3.** A crowd; a coming together.	**mel·lif·lu·ous** (mə-lĭf′lōō-əs) *adj.* Smoothly or sweetly flowing. -**mel·lif′lu·ous·ly**, *adv.* -**mel·lif′lu·ous·ness**, *n.*	**re·flex** (rē′flĕks′) *n.* An involuntary response to a stimulus.	**su·per·flu·ous** (sōō-pûr′flōō-əs) *adj.* Being more than is necessary, wanted, or required. -**su·per′flu·ous·ly**, *adv.* -**su·per′flu·ous·ness**, *n.*
in·flux (ĭn′flŭks) *n.* A flowing in or mass arrival.	**ef·flu·ent** (ĕf′lōō-ənt) *n.* The outflow of something, especially a stream from a body of water, an outflow from a sewer, or a discharge of waste from a factory.	**fluc·tu·ate** (flŭk′chōō-āt′) *v.* **-at·ed, -at·ing.** To change up and down or back and forth irregularly; waver.	**fluent** (flōō′ənt) *adj.* **1.** Spoken or written easily. **2.** Able to speak or write smoothly and effortlessly. **3.** Flowing smoothly. -**flu′en·cy**, *n.*	**gen·u·flect** (jĕn′yə-flĕkt′) *v.* To bend the knee, or touch the knee to the floor, as in respect or worship.

Lesson 11	Lesson 11	Lesson 11	Lesson 11	Lesson 11
laissez faire (lĕs′ā fâr′) *adj.* Favoring or practicing a policy of non-interference in the affairs of others. **laissez faire**, *n.*	**nou·veau riche** (nōō′vō rēsh′) *n., pl.* **nouveaux riches** (nōō′vō rēsh′) A person who is newly rich, especially one who shows off the wealth.	**par ex·cel·lence** (pär ĕk-sə-läns′) *adj.* Being an example of excellence.	**savoir-faire** (săv′wär-fâr′) *n.* The ability to say or do the right thing in any situation.	**tête-à-tête** (tāt′ə-tāt′, tĕt′-tĕt′) *n.* A private conversation between two people. *-adv. & adj.* For or of two people in intimate privacy.
au con·traire (ō-kŏn-trâr′) *adv.* On the contrary.	**coup d'é·tat** (kōō dā-tä′) *n., pl.* **-coups d'é·tat.** A sudden overthrow of the government.	**é·lan** (ā-län′) *n.* **1.** Enthusiasm; vigor. **2.** Style; flair.	**es·prit de corps** (ĕ-sprē′ də kôr′) *n.* A sense of pride, loyalty, unity, and devotion to a cause among the members of a group.	**faux pas** (fō pä′) *n., pl.* **faux pas** (fō päz′). An embarrassing social mistake.

Lesson 10	Lesson 10	Lesson 10	Lesson 10	Lesson 10
in·trin·sic (ĭn-trĭn′zĭk, -sĭk) *adj.* Belonging to the real nature of a thing; essential; inherent. -**in·trin′si·cal·ly**, *adv.*	**o·vert** (ō-vûrt′, ō′vûrt′) *adj.* Open; observable; not hidden. -**o·vert′ly**, *adv.* -**o·vert′ness**, *n.*	**rail** (rāl) *v.* To complain violently or bitterly. -**rail′er**, *n.*	**rec·on·cile** (rĕk′ən-sīl′) *v.* **-ciled, -cil·ing. 1.** To make agree, consistent, or compatible. **2.** To make friendly again. -**rec′on·cil′a·ble**, *adj.*	**un·prec·e·dent·ed** (ŭn-prĕs′ĭ-dĕn′tĭd) *adj.* Not having a previous example; unheard of. -**un·prec′e·dent′ed·ly**, *adv.*
as·pire (ə-spīr′) *v.* **-pired, -pir·ing.** To be ambitious; desire; aim. -**as·pir′er**, *n.* -**as·pir′ing·ly**, *adv.*	**dense** (dĕns) *adj.* **dens·er, dens·est.** Packed closely together; thick; compact. -**dense′ly**, *adv.* -**dense′ness**, *n.*	**em·u·late** (ĕm′yə-lāt′) *v.* **-lat·ed, -lat·ing.** To imitate in order to equal or surpass. -**em·u·la′tor**, *n.*	**gro·tesque** (grō-tĕsk′) *adj.* **1.** Deformed, distorted, odd, or unnatural in appearance. **2.** Absurd; ridiculous. -**gro·tesque′ly**, *adv.* -**gro·tesque′ness**, *n.*	**in·ex·tri·ca·bly** (ĭn-ĕk′strĭ-kə-blē, ĭn ĭk-strĭk′ə-blē) *adv.* Unavoidably; inescapably. -**in·ex′tri·ca·bil′i·ty**, *n.* -**in·ex′tri·ca·ble**, *adj.*

Lesson 12	inflexible	Lesson 12	influx	Lesson 12	mellifluous	Lesson 12	reflex	Lesson 12	superfluous
Lesson 12	confluence	Lesson 12	effluent	Lesson 12	fluctuate	Lesson 12	fluent	Lesson 12	genuflect
Lesson 11	laissez faire	Lesson 11	nouveau riche	Lesson 11	par excellence	Lesson 11	savoir-faire	Lesson 11	tête-à-tête
Lesson 11	au contraire	Lesson 11	coup d'état	Lesson 11	élan	Lesson 11	esprit de corps	Lesson 11	faux pas
Lesson 10	intrinsic	Lesson 10	overt	Lesson 10	rail	Lesson 10	reconcile	Lesson 10	unprecedented
Lesson 10	aspire	Lesson 10	dense	Lesson 10	emulate	Lesson 10	grotesque	Lesson 10	inextricably

Lesson 15

eu·lo·gize
(yōo′lə-jīz′) v. -gized, -giz·ing. To praise highly (especially a person who has just died) in speech or writing. -eu′lo·gy, n.

Lesson 15

eu·phe·mism
(yōo′fə-mĭz′əm) n. The use of a mild or less direct word or phrase in place of one considered blunt or offensive. eu′phe·mis′tic, adj.

Lesson 15

eu·pho·ri·a
(yōo-fôr′ē-ə, -fōr′-) n. A strong feeling of well-being or happiness. -eu·phor′ic, adj. -eu·phor′i·cal·ly, adv.

Lesson 15

eu·tha·na·sia
(yōo′thə-nā′zhə, -zhē-ə) n. The painless killing of a person suffering from an incurable disease.

Lesson 15

mas·tec·to·my
(mă-stĕk′tə-mē) n., pl. -mies. Surgical removal of the breast.

Lesson 15

ap·pen·dec·to·my
(ăp′ən-dĕk′tə-mē) n., pl. -mies. The surgical removal of the appendix.

Lesson 15

ec·cen·tric
(ĭk-sĕn′trĭk, ĕk-) adj. Not conforming to normal or usual behavior; odd; peculiar. -ec·cen′tri·cal·ly, adv.

Lesson 15

e·clec·tic
(ĭ-klĕk′tĭk) adj. Selected or made up of elements from various sources. -e·clec′ti·cal·ly, adv.

Lesson 15

e·clipse
(ĭ-klĭps′) n. A partial or complete hiding of one celestial body by another. -v. -e·clipsed, -e·clips·ing. To overshadow.

Lesson 15

ec·stat·ic
(ĕk-stăt′ĭk) adj. Overwhelmed with intense joy or delight. -ec′sta·sy, n. -ec·stat′i·cal·ly, adv.

Lesson 14

dis·sem·i·nate
(dĭ-sĕm′ə-nāt′) v. -nat·ed, -nat·ing. To scatter widely; spread about. -dis·sem′i·na′tion, n.

Lesson 14

lig·a·ture
(lĭg′ə-chŏŏr′, -chər) n. Something that is used for tying or binding.

Lesson 14

pe·riph·er·y
(pə-rĭf′ə-rē) n., pl. -ies. 1. The edge or border of an area. 2. The surrounding area.

Lesson 14

per·me·ate
(pûr′mē-āt′) v. -at·ed, -at·ing. To spread throughout; penetrate through. -per′me·a′tion, n.

Lesson 14

per·va·sive
(pər-vā′sĭv, -zĭv) adj. Tending to spread throughout. -per·va′sive·ly, adv. -per·va′sive·ness, n. -per·vade′, v.

Lesson 14

a·dul·ter·ate
(ə-dŭl′tə-rāt′) v. -at·ed, -at·ing. To make impure or inferior by adding poor or improper substances. -a·dul′ter·a′tion, n.

Lesson 14

a·mal·ga·mate
(ə-măl′gə-māt′) v. -mat·ed, -mat·ing. To mix, combine, or merge. -a·mal′ga·ma′tion, n.

Lesson 14

co·a·lesce
(kō′ə-lĕs′) v. 1. -lesced, -lesc·ing. To unite to form a whole. -co′a·les′cence, n. -co′a·les′cent, adj.

Lesson 14

cor·re·late
(kôr′ə-lāt′, kŏr′-) v. -lat·ed, -lat·ing. 1. To put in a mutual relation. 2. To show a connection between. -cor′re·la′tion, n.

Lesson 14

dif·fuse
(dĭ-fyōoz′) v. -fused, -fus·ing. To scatter widely; spread out. -adj. (dĭ-fyōos′) Widely spread or scattered.

Lesson 13

in·vi·o·la·ble
(ĭn-vī′ə-lə-bəl) adj. 1. Not to be violated or profaned. 2. Indestructible. -in·vi·o·la·bly, adv.

Lesson 13

mol·li·fy
(mŏl′ə-fī′) v. -fied, -fy·ing, -fies. 1. To soothe anger or hostility. 2. To make less intense or violent. -mol′li·fi′a·ble, adj.

Lesson 13

ob·vi·ate
(ŏb′vē-āt′) v. -at·ed, -at·ing. To anticipate and prevent. -ob′vi·a′tion, n. -ob′vi·a′tor, n.

Lesson 13

prov·o·ca·tion
(prŏv′ə-kā′shən) n. Something that incites anger or stirs to action. -pro·voke′, v.

Lesson 13

re·dress
(rĭ-drĕs′) n. Compensation or satisfaction for a wrong. -v. To correct; remedy; to compensate. -re·dress′er, re·dres′sor, n.

Lesson 13

ac·cost
(ə-kôst′, ə-kŏst′) v. To approach and speak to in a hostile or aggressive manner.

Lesson 13

ac·qui·esce
(ăk′wē-ĕs′) v. -esced, -esc·ing. To consent silently or without protest; assent.

Lesson 13

du·ress
(dōo-rĕs′, dyōo-) n. 1. Constraint by force or threat. 2. Imprisonment.

Lesson 13

em·bold·en
(ĕm-bōl′dən) v. To make bold; encourage.

Lesson 13

ex·tant
(ĕk′stənt, ĕk-stănt′) adj. Still existing; not lost, destroyed, or extinct.

Lesson 15	Lesson 15	Lesson 14	Lesson 14	Lesson 13	Lesson 13
eulogize	appendectomy	disseminate	adulterate	inviolable	accost
euphemism	eccentric	ligature	amalgamate	mollify	acquiesce
euphoria	eclectic	periphery	coalesce	obviate	duress
euthanasia	eclipse	permeate	correlate	provocation	embolden
mastectomy	ecstatic	pervasive	diffuse	redress	extant

Lesson 18

e·dict
(ē′dĭkt) *n.* An official decree or proclamation issued by a ruler or other person having authority.

el·o·cu·tion
(ĕl′ə-kyōō′shən) *n.* **1.** The art of public speaking. **2.** The style or manner of speaking or reading in public. **-el′o·cu′tion·ist**, *n.*

in·ter·dict
(ĭn′tər-dĭkt′) *v.* To prohibit or forbid, especially officially. *-n.* (ĭn′tər-dĭkt′) An official prohibition. **-in′ter·dic′tion**, *n.*

lo·qua·cious
(lō-kwā′shəs) *adj.* Very talkative. **-lo·qua′cious·ly**, *adv.* **-lo·qua′cious·ness**, *n.*

mal·e·dic·tion
(măl′ĭ-dĭk′shən) *n.* **1.** A curse. **2.** Slander. **-mal′e·dic′to·ry**, *adj.*

Lesson 18

cir·cum·lo·cu·tion
(sûr′kəm-lō-kyōō′shən) *n.* A roundabout or indirect way of speaking; wordiness. **-cir′cum·loc′u·to′ri·ly**, *adv.* **-cir′cum·loc′u·to′ry**, *adj.*

col·lo·qui·um
(kə-lō′kwē-əm) *n.*, *pl.* **-qui·ums** or **-qui·a.** An academic conference or meeting on some subject.

con·tra·dict
(kŏn′trə-dĭkt′) *v.* **1.** To say the opposite of. **2.** To declare to be untrue. **-con′tra·dic′tion**, *n.*

dic·tate
(dĭk′tāt′, dĭk-tāt′) *v.* **-tat·ed, -tat·ing. 1.** To say or read aloud to be recorded by another. **2.** To command. *-n.* A command.

dic·tum
(dĭk′təm) *n.*, *pl.* **-ta** (tə) or **-tums.** A formal official statement or opinion.

Lesson 17

de·ride
(dĭ-rīd′) *v.* **-rid·ed, rid·ing.** To laugh at in contempt or scorn; ridicule. **-de·rid′er**, *n.* **-de·rid′ing·ly**, *adv.*

im·peach
(ĭm-pēch′) *v.* **-peach·es. 1.** To bring formal charges against a public official. **2.** To discredit (a person's honor). **-im·peach′ment**, *n.*

in·nu·en·do
(ĭn′yōō-ĕn′dō) *n.*, *pl.* **-does.** A hint or indirect suggestion, usually meant to damage a person's reputation.

re·mon·strate
(rĭ-mŏn′strāt′) *v.* **-strat·ed, -strat·ing.** To plead or reason in protest; to present objections against something. **-re·mon′stra·tive**, *adj.*

up·braid
(ŭp-brād′) *v.* To scold sharply; reproach. **-up·braid′er**, *n.* **-up·braid′ing·ly**, *adv.*

Lesson 17

ac·ri·mo·ni·ous
(ăk′rə-mō′nē-əs) *adj.* Bitter or sarcastic in language, temper, manner, or tone. **-ac′ri·mo′ny**, *n.* **-ac′ri·mo′ni·ous·ly**, *adv.*

as·per·sion
(ə-spûr′zhən, -shən) *n.* A damaging or untrue remark; slander.

cen·sure
(sĕn′shər) *v.* **-sured, -sur·ing.** To criticize harshly; blame; condemn. *-n.* **1.** A strong disapproval. **2.** An official criticism. **-cen′sur·er**, *n.*

cri·tique
(krĭ-tēk′) *n.* A critical review, especially one dealing with works of art or literature. *-v.* To review or discuss critically.

de·fame
(dĭ-fām′) *v.* **-famed, -fam·ing.** To attack the reputation or good name of; slander or libel. **-def′a·ma′tion**, *n.*

Lesson 16

gam·bol
(găm′bəl) *v.* **-boled, -bol·ing** or **-bolled, -bol·ling.** To jump or skip playfully; frolic. *-n.* A playful jumping or skipping about.

pru·dent
(prōōd′nt) *adj.* **1.** Wise and sensible in handling practical matters. **2.** Careful or cautious in conduct. **-pru′dent·ly**, *adv.*

rig·or·ous
(rĭg′ər-əs) *adj.* **1.** Strict; inflexible. **2.** Severe; harsh; difficult. **-rig′or·ous·ly**, *adv.* **-rig′or·ous·ness**, *n.*

suc·cu·lent
(sŭk′yə-lənt) *adj.* **1.** Juicy. **2.** Having thick, fleshy leaves and stems that hold water. **-suc′cu·lence, suc′cu·len·cy**, *n.* **-suc′cu·lent·ly**, *adv.*

taw·ny
(tô′nē) *adj.* **-ni·er, -ni·est.** Brownish-yellow; tan. **-taw′ni·ness**, *n.*

Lesson 16

a·grar·i·an
(ə-grâr′ē-ən) *adj.* **1.** Relating to agricultural or farming matters. **2.** Relating to land and its ownership or use.

a·me·lio·rate
(ə-mēl′yə-rāt′) *v.* **-rat·ed, -rat·ing.** To make or become better; improve. **-a·me′lio·ra′tion**, *n.*

com·mis·sar·y
(kŏm′ĭ-sĕr′ē) *n.*, *pl.* **-ies. 1.** A place to eat; cafeteria. **2.** A store where food and supplies are sold, as in an army camp.

con·ster·na·tion
(kŏn′stər-nā′shən) *n.* A feeling of alarm or dismay characterized by confusion or fear. **-con′ster·nate**, *v.*

ex·cise
(ĭk-sīz′) *v.* **-cised, -cis·ing.** To remove by cutting out. **-ex·ci′sion**, *n.*

Lesson 18	edict	Lesson 18	circumlocution
Lesson 18	elocution	Lesson 18	colloquium
Lesson 18	interdict	Lesson 18	contradict
Lesson 18	loquacious	Lesson 18	dictate
Lesson 18	malediction	Lesson 18	dictum
Lesson 17	deride	Lesson 17	acrimonious
Lesson 17	impeach	Lesson 17	aspersion
Lesson 17	innuendo	Lesson 17	censure
Lesson 17	remonstrate	Lesson 17	critique
Lesson 17	upbraid	Lesson 17	defame
Lesson 16	gambol	Lesson 16	agrarian
Lesson 16	prudent	Lesson 16	ameliorate
Lesson 16	rigorous	Lesson 16	commissary
Lesson 16	succulent	Lesson 16	consternation
Lesson 16	tawny	Lesson 16	excise

Lesson 21	Lesson 21	Lesson 21	Lesson 21	Lesson 21
e·voc·a·tive (ĭ-vŏk'ə-tĭv) *adj.* Tending or having the power to call forth or bring out, especially memories or emotions.	**ir·rev·o·ca·ble** (ĭ-rĕv'ə-kə-bəl) *adj.* Not to be reversed, withdrawn, retracted, or recalled. **-ir·rev'o·ca·bly,** *adv.*	**proc·la·ma·tion** (prŏk'lə-mā'shən) *n.* Something that is declared publicly, especially an official public announcement.	**rec·la·ma·tion** (rĕk'lə-mā'shən) *n.* A restoration or recovery to usefulness or a better state.	**vouch** (vouch) *v.* 1. To give assurance or one's word or guarantee. 2. To serve as evidence or guarantee.

Lesson 21	Lesson 21	Lesson 21	Lesson 21	Lesson 21
av·o·ca·tion (ăv'ō-kā'shən) *n.* Something done in addition to one's regular occupation; hobby. **-av'o·ca'tion·al,** *adj.*	**claim·ant** (klā'mənt) *n.* A person who makes a claim.	**clam·or·ous** (klăm'ər-əs) *adj.* 1. Noisy and loud. 2. Loudly demanding. **-clam'or,** *n.* **-clam'or·ous·ly,** *adv.*	**de·claim** (dĭ-klām') *v.* To speak loudly and forcefully. **-de·claim'er,** *n.*	**e·quiv·o·cate** (ĭ-kwĭv'ə-kāt') *v.* **-cat·ed, -cat·ing.** 1. To use ambiguous language. 2. To avoid making an exact statement. **-equiv'o·ca'tion,** *n.*

Lesson 20	Lesson 20	Lesson 20	Lesson 20	Lesson 20
dis·so·nance (dĭs'ə-nəns) *n.* 1. A harsh or unpleasant combination of sounds; discord. 2. A lack of agreement. **-dis'so·nant,** *adj.*	**dul·cet** (dŭl'sĭt) *adj.* Soothing or pleasing to the ear; melodious.	**li·bret·to** (lĭ-brĕt'ō) *n., pl.* **-bret·tos** or **-bret·ti** (-brĕt'ē). The text or words of an opera or dramatic musical work.	**mo·tif** (mō-tēf') *n.* A recurring theme, idea, or subject in art, literature, music, or drama.	**sur·re·al·is·tic** (sə-rē'ə-lĭs'tĭk) *adj.* Having a dreamlike or unreal quality. **-sur·re·al·is'ti·cal·ly,** *adv.*

Lesson 20	Lesson 20	Lesson 20	Lesson 20	Lesson 20
a cap·pel·la (ä'kə-pĕl'ə) *adv.* Without instrumental accompaniment.	**ab·stract** (ăb-străkt', ăb'străkt') *adj.* 1. Thought of apart from concrete objects. 2. Relating to a style of art that does not represent real form.	**aes·thet·ic** (ĕs-thĕt'ĭk) *adj.* 1. Sensitive to art and beauty. 2. Artistic. 3. Relating to art and beauty. **-aes·thet'i·cal·ly,** *adv.*	**a·vant-garde** (ä'vänt-gärd', ăv'änt-) *n.* People who use or experiment with new styles, techniques, or ideas, especially in the arts.	**ca·coph·o·ny** (kə-kŏf'ə-nē) *n., pl.* **-nies.** A harsh, jarring, or unpleasant sound; discord. **-ca·coph'o·nous,** *adj.*

Lesson 19	Lesson 19	Lesson 19	Lesson 19	Lesson 19
o·ri·ent (ôr'ē-ĕnt, ōr'-) *v.* 1. To place or position with reference to a certain point. 2. To adjust to new surroundings or situations.	**pal·ette** (păl'ĭt) *n.* 1. A board on which artists place and mix their paints. 2. The colors used for a painting. 3. A range of choices.	**pidg·in** (pĭj'ən) *n.* A simplified mixture of languages used by people who speak different languages.	**pro·cliv·i·ty** (prō-klĭv'ĭ-tē) *n., pl.* **-ties.** A natural tendency; inclination.	**sub·tle** (sŭt'l) *adj.* 1. So faint or slight as to be not obvious. 2. Capable of seeing or understanding fine distinctions. **-sub'tly,** *adv.*

Lesson 19	Lesson 19	Lesson 19	Lesson 19	Lesson 19
cru·cial (krōō'shəl) *adj.* Extremely important; decisive; critical. **-cru'cial·ly,** *adv.*	**dy·nam·ic** (dī-năm'ĭk) *adj.* 1. Characterized by change or activity. 2. Energetic; forceful. **-dy·nam'i·cal·ly,** *adv.*	**her·e·sy** (hĕr'ĭ-sē) *n., pl.* **-sies. 1.** A religious belief that is opposed to accepted beliefs. 2. Any belief opposed to the established beliefs or customs.	**in·nate** (ĭ-nāt', ĭn'āt') *adj.* Possessed at birth; natural; inborn. **-in·nate'ly,** *adv.* **-in·nate'ness,** *n.*	**lin·guist** (lĭng'gwĭst) *n.* 1. An expert in the study of language. 2. A person skilled in several languages. **-lin·guis'tics,** *n.*

Lesson 21 evocative	Lesson 21 avocation	Lesson 20 dissonance	Lesson 20 a cappella	Lesson 19 orient	Lesson 19 crucial
Lesson 21 irrevocable	Lesson 21 claimant	Lesson 20 dulcet	Lesson 20 abstract	Lesson 19 palette	Lesson 19 dynamic
Lesson 21 proclamation	Lesson 21 clamorous	Lesson 20 libretto	Lesson 20 aesthetic	Lesson 19 pidgin	Lesson 19 heresy
Lesson 21 reclamation	Lesson 21 declaim	Lesson 20 motif	Lesson 20 avant-garde	Lesson 19 proclivity	Lesson 19 innate
Lesson 21 vouch	Lesson 21 equivocate	Lesson 20 surrealistic	Lesson 20 cacophony	Lesson 19 subtle	Lesson 19 linguist

Lesson 24	Lesson 24	Lesson 23	Lesson 23	Lesson 22	Lesson 22
mort·gage (môr′gĭj) n. 1. The pledge of property to a creditor as security for a debt. 2. The deed that gives the terms of such a pledge.	**am·or·tize** (ăm′ər-tīz′, ə-môr′-) v. -tized, -tiz·ing. To pay (a debt) by making payments at periodic intervals.	**par·si·mo·ny** (pär′sə-mō′nē) n. A tendency to be excessively careful in spending money; stinginess. -par·si·mo′ni·ous, adj.	**av·a·rice** (ăv′ə-rĭs) n. Greed for money or possessions. -av·a·ri′cious, adj.	**stead·fast** (stĕd′făst′, -fəst) adj. 1. Firm; steady. 2. Faithful; unwavering. -stead′fast′ly, adv. -stead′fast′ness, n.	**a·kin** (ə-kĭn′) adj. 1. Having similar qualities or character. 2. Related by blood.
mor·ti·fy (môr′tə-fī′) v. -fied, -fy·ing, -fies. To shame, humiliate, or embarrass.	**im·mor·tal·ize** (ĭ-môr′tl-īz′) v. -ized, -iz·ing. To make remembered, everlasting, or famous for the future.	**prod·i·gal** (prŏd′ĭ-gəl) adj. Foolishly or wastefully extravagant.	**glut·ton·ous** (glŭt′n-əs) adj. Given to eating too much or greedily. -glut′ton, n. -glut′tony, n. -glut′ton·ous·ly, adv.	**trans·fig·ure** (trăns-fĭg′yər) v. -ured, -ur·ing. To change the outward appearance of.	**in·cho·ate** (ĭn-kō′ĭt) adj. In an early stage; just begun. -in·cho′ate·ly, adv. -in·cho′ate·ness, n.
mor·tu·ary (môr′chōō-ĕr′ē) n., pl. -ies. A place where dead bodies are kept before burial or cremation.	**mor·bid** (môr′bĭd) adj. 1. Overly preoccupied with death, disease, or decay. 2. Sickly. 3. Gruesome; grisly. -mor′bid·ly, adv.	**prof·li·gate** (prŏf′lĭ-gĭt, -gāt′) adj. 1. Recklessly wasteful. 2. Utterly immoral. -prof′li·ga·cy, n. -prof′li·gate·ly, adv.	**in·tem·per·ate** (ĭn-tĕm′pər-ĭt, -prĭt) adj. Without restraint or self-control; excessive. -in·tem′per·ate·ly, adv.	**un·wary** (ŭn-wâr′ē) adj. -i·er, -i·est. Not cautious, careful, or watchful. -un·war′i·ly, adv. -un·war′i·ness, n.	**in·del·i·ble** (ĭn-dĕl′ə-bəl) adj. Impossible to erase, remove, or wash out; permanent. -in·del′i·bil′i·ty, n. -in·del′i·bly, adv.
post·mor·tem (pōst-môr′təm) adj. Happening or done after death. -n. A medical examination of a dead body.	**mor·dant** (môr′dnt) adj. 1. Biting or sarcastic. 2. Bitingly painful. -mor′dan·cy, n. -mor′dant·ly, adv.	**ra·pac·i·ty** (rə-păs′ĭ-tē) n. 1. Willingness to take by force or plunder. 2. The quality of being greedy. -ra·pa′cious, adj.	**in·un·date** (ĭn′ŭn-dāt′, ĭn′ən-) v. -dat·ed, -dat·ing. 1. To cover with water, as in a flood. 2. To overwhelm. -in·un·da′tion, n.	**var·i·a·ble** (vâr′ē-ə-bəl, văr′-) adj. Likely to change; changeable. -var′i·a·ble·ness, n. -var′i·a·bly, adv.	**plumb** (plŭm) v. To examine closely in order to discover the contents or facts of.
re·morse (rĭ-môrs′) n. A deep, painful feeling of regret, guilt, or sorrow for wrongdoing. -re·morse′ful, adj. -re·morse′ful·ness, n.	**mor·i·bund** (môr′ə-bŭnd′, mŏr′-) adj. Near death; dying. -mor′i·bun′di·ty, n. -mor′i·bund′ly, adv.	**re·plete** (rĭ-plēt′) adj. 1. Abundantly supplied. 2. Filled with food. -re·plete′ness, n.	**ob·sess** (əb-sĕs′, ŏb-) v. -sess·es. To occupy or trouble the mind excessively. -obses′sion, n. -ob·ses′sive, adj.	**vie** (vī) v. vied, vy·ing (vī′ing), vies. To compete for superiority.	**pris·tine** (prĭs′tēn′, prĭ-stēn′) adj. 1. Unspoiled; pure; uncorrupted. 2. Original; primitive. -pris′tine′ly, adv.

Lesson 24 mortgage	Lesson 24 mortify	Lesson 24 mortuary	Lesson 24 postmortem	Lesson 24 remorse
Lesson 24 amortize	Lesson 24 immortalize	Lesson 24 morbid	Lesson 24 mordant	Lesson 24 moribund
Lesson 23 parsimony	Lesson 23 prodigal	Lesson 23 profligate	Lesson 23 rapacity	Lesson 23 replete
Lesson 23 avarice	Lesson 23 gluttonous	Lesson 23 intemperate	Lesson 23 inundate	Lesson 23 obsess
Lesson 22 steadfast	Lesson 22 transfigure	Lesson 22 unwary	Lesson 22 variable	Lesson 22 vie
Lesson 22 akin	Lesson 22 inchoate	Lesson 22 indelible	Lesson 22 plumb	Lesson 22 pristine

Lesson 25

advocate
(ăd'və-kāt') v. -cat-ed, -cat-ing. To plead in favor of. -n. (ăd'və-kĭt) One who defends a cause. -ad'vo-ca-cy, n.

Lesson 25

arable
(ăr'ə-bəl) adj. Suitable for cultivation by plowing. -ar'a-bil'i-ty, n.

Lesson 25

edifice
(ĕd'ə-fĭs) n. A building, especially a large and imposing one.

Lesson 25

heyday
(hā'dā') n. The period of greatest success, power, strength, popularity, etc; prime.

Lesson 25

intimidate
(ĭn-tĭm'ĭ-dāt') v. -dat-ed, -dat-ing. To frighten; to make timid. -in-tim'i-da'tion, n. -in-tim'i-da'tor, n.

Lesson 25

notorious
(nō-tôr'ē-əs, -tōr'-) adj. Well-known, usually unfavorably. -no-to'ri-ous-ly, adv. -no-to'ri-ous-ness, n.

Lesson 25

nutriment
(nōō'trə-mənt, nyōō'-) n. Anything that nourishes; food.

Lesson 25

obsolete
(ŏb'sə-lēt', ŏb'sə-lēt') adj. 1. No longer in use. 2. Out-of-date.

Lesson 25

perpetuate
(pər-pĕch'ōō-āt') v. -at-ed, -at-ing. To make to last or continue for a very long time. -per-pet'u-a'tion, n.

Lesson 25

predilection
(prĕd'1-ĕk'shən, prēd'-) n. A special liking for something; preference.

Lesson 26

cataclysm
(kăt'ə-klĭz'əm) n. Any violent upheaval or sudden change. -cat-a-clys'mic, adj.

Lesson 26

decadence
(dĕk'ə-dəns, dĭ-kād'ns) n. A period, condition, or process of decline or decay as in morals, art, or literature. -dec'a-dent, adj.

Lesson 26

decimate
(dĕs'ə-māt') v. -mat-ed, -mat-ing. To destroy or kill a large number or part of. -dec'i-ma'tion, n.

Lesson 26

depredate
(dĕp'rĭ-dāt') v. -dat-ed, -dat-ing. To rob; ransack; plunder. -dep're-da'tion, n. -dep're-da'tor, n.

Lesson 26

expunge
(ĭk-spŭnj') v. -punged, -pung-ing. To delete or erase. -ex-pung'er, n.

Lesson 26

interpolate
(ĭn-tûr'pə-lāt') v. -lat-ed, -lat-ing. 1. To change (a text) by inserting new words or material. 2. To insert new material.

Lesson 26

obliterate
(ə-blĭt'ə-rāt', ō-blĭt'-) v. -at-ed, -at-ing. 1. To destroy completely. 2. To blot out; erase. -o-blit'er-a'tion, n.

Lesson 26

putrefaction
(pyōō'trə-făk'shən) n. The decay of organic matter resulting in the formation of foul-smelling matter. -pu'tre-fy, v.

Lesson 26

stagnate
(stăg'nāt') v. -nat-ed, -nat-ing. 1. To become motionless. 2. To become foul from standing still. 3. To stop growing. -stag-na'tion, n.

Lesson 26

wane
(wān) v. waned, wan-ing. 1. To decrease gradually. 2. To decline in power, importance, or influence.

Lesson 27

carnage
(kär'nĭj) n. A bloody and massive slaughter, as in battle; massacre.

Lesson 27

carnal
(kär'nəl) adj. 1. Relating to the body or flesh. 2. Worldly; not spiritual. -car'nal-ly, adv.

Lesson 27

carnivore
(kär'nə-vôr', -vōr') n. An animal that eats flesh. -car-niv'o-rous, adj.

Lesson 27

clairvoyant
(klâr-voi'ənt) adj. Supposedly able to see or know about things that cannot be perceived by the senses. -n. A clairvoyant person.

Lesson 27

improvise
(ĭm'prə-vīz') v. -vised, -vis-ing. 1. To compose or perform without preparation. 2. To make or provide from the materials at hand.

Lesson 27

incarnate
(ĭn-kär'nĭt) adj. Embodied in human form; personified. -v. (ĭn-kär'nāt') To personify. -in'car-na'tion, n.

Lesson 27

invidious
(ĭn-vĭd'ē-əs) adj. Arousing or likely to arouse ill will or hatred; offensive. -in-vid'i-ous-ly, adv.

Lesson 27

providence
(prŏv'ĭ-dəns, -dĕns) n. 1. The care, guidance, or control by a deity; divine guidance. 2. Providence. God.

Lesson 27

reincarnation
(rē'ĭn-kär-nā'shən) n. 1. A rebirth or reappearance in another form. 2. The rebirth of the soul in a different body. -re'in-car'nate, v.

Lesson 27

visage
(vĭz'ĭj) n. The face or facial appearance of a person.

Lesson 27	Lesson 27	Lesson 27	Lesson 27	Lesson 27
incarnate	invidious	providence	reincarnation	visage
Lesson 27	**Lesson 27**	**Lesson 27**	**Lesson 27**	**Lesson 27**
carnage	carnal	carnivore	clairvoyant	improvise
Lesson 26	**Lesson 26**	**Lesson 26**	**Lesson 26**	**Lesson 26**
interpolate	obliterate	putrefaction	stagnate	wane
Lesson 26	**Lesson 26**	**Lesson 26**	**Lesson 26**	**Lesson 26**
cataclysm	decadence	decimate	depredate	expunge
Lesson 25	**Lesson 25**	**Lesson 25**	**Lesson 25**	**Lesson 25**
notorious	nutriment	obsolete	perpetuate	predilection
Lesson 25	**Lesson 25**	**Lesson 25**	**Lesson 25**	**Lesson 25**
advocate	arable	edifice	heyday	intimidate

Lesson 30

re·pel·lent (rĭ-pĕl′ənt) *adj.* **1.** Tending to drive away. **2.** Causing dislike or distaste. –*n.* Something that wards something off or keeps it away.

Lesson 30

com·pul·so·ry (kəm-pŭl′sə-rē) *adj.* Required; enforced. -**compul′so·ri·ly,** *adv.*

Lesson 30

vi·a·ble (vī′ə-bəl) *adj.* **1.** Capable of living and developing. **2.** Workable; practicable. -**vi′a·bil′i·ty,** *n.* -**vi′a·bly,** *adv.*

Lesson 30

con·viv·i·al (kən-vĭv′ē·əl) *adj.* **1.** Fond of eating, drinking, and good company; sociable. **2.** Festive. -**con·viv′i·al′i·ty,** *n.* -**con·viv′i·al·ly,** *adv.*

Lesson 30

vic·tu·al (vĭt′l) *n.* Food for human consumption. –*v.* -**ualed, -ual·ing,** or -**ualled, -ual·ling.** To supply with food.

Lesson 30

dis·pel (dĭ-spĕl′) *v.* -**pelled, -pel·ling.** To drive away; cause to disappear.

Lesson 30

vi·tal·i·ty (vī-tăl′ĭ-tē) *n., pl.* -**ties.** **1.** The power to live, grow, or develop. **2.** Mental or physical vigor; energy.

Lesson 30

im·pel (ĭm-pĕl′) *v.* -**pelled, pel·ling.** **1.** To drive or force to action; compel. **2.** To propel or drive forward.

Lesson 30

vi·va·cious (vĭ-vā′shəs, vī-) *adj.* Full of life and spirit; animated. -**viva′cious·ly,** *adv.* -**viva′cious·ness,** *n.*

Lesson 30

pul·sate (pŭl′sāt′) *v.* -**sat·ed, -sat·ing.** **1.** To expand and contract rhythmically; throb. **2.** To vibrate; quiver.

Lesson 29

mal·le·a·ble (măl′ē-ə-bəl) *adj.* **1.** Able to be hammered or pressed into various shapes without breaking. **2.** Adaptable. -**mal′le·a·bil′i·ty,** *n.*

Lesson 29

met·a·mor·pho·sis (mĕt′ə-môr′fə-sĭs) *n., pl.* -**ses** (-sēz) **1.** A transformation, as if by magic. **2.** A complete change in appearance, character, etc.

Lesson 29

mod·u·late (mŏj′ə-lāt′) *v.* -**lat·ed, -lat·ing.** **1.** To vary the pitch, tone, or volume of. **2.** To regulate or adjust. -**mod′u·la′tion,** *n.*

Lesson 29

vac·il·late (văs′ə-lāt′) *v.* -**lat·ed, -lat·ing.** **1.** To waver in mind or feeling; to be indecisive. **2.** To sway to and fro; waver. -**vac′il·la′tion,** *n.*

Lesson 29

vol·a·tile (vŏl′ə-tl, -tīl) *adj.* **1.** Changeable. **2.** Tending to violence; explosive. -**vol′a·til′i·ty,** *n.*

Lesson 29

ca·pri·cious (kə-prĭsh′əs, -prē′shəs) *adj.* Tending to change suddenly for no apparent reason; unpredictable. -**capri′cious·ly,** *adv.*

Lesson 29

de·sul·to·ry (dĕs′əl-tôr′ē, -tōr′ē, dĕz′-) *adj.* Jumping from one thing to another; disconnected. -**des′ul·to′ri·ly,** *adv.*

Lesson 29

e·phem·er·al (ĭ-fĕm′ər-əl) *adj.* Lasting only a short time; short-lived. -**e·phem′er·al·ly,** *adv.*

Lesson 29

im·mu·ta·ble (ĭ-myōō′tə-bəl) *adj.* Unchangeable. -**im·mu′ta·bil′i·ty, im·mu′ta·ble·ness,** *n.* -**im·mu′ta·bly,** *adv.*

Lesson 29

in·vet·er·ate (ĭn-vĕt′ər-ĭt) *adj.* **1.** Firmly established; deep-rooted. **2.** Confirmed in an ingrained habit; habitual. -**invet′er·ate·ly,** *adv.*

Lesson 28

prim·i·tive (prĭm′ĭ-tĭv) *adj.* **1.** Characterized by simplicity; unsophisticated. **2.** Relating to an early or original stage.

Lesson 28

scru·pu·lous (skrōō′pyə-ləs) *adj.* **1.** Very careful of details; painstaking; exact. **2.** Principled; honest. -**scru′pu·lous·ly,** *adv.*

Lesson 28

suf·fuse (sə-fyōōz′) *v.* -**fused, -fus·ing.** To spread through, as with a light, color, emotion, etc. -**suf·fu′sion,** *n.*

Lesson 28

tran·sient (trăn′shənt, -zhənt, -zē·ənt) *adj.* Lasting only a short time; not permanent. -**tran′sience,** *n.* -**tran′sient·ly,** *adv.*

Lesson 28

vi·gnette (vĭn-yĕt′) *n.* **1.** A short scene or incident. **2.** An ornamental design used at the beginning or end of a book or chapter. **3.** A short literary sketch.

Lesson 28

ap·o·gee (ăp′ə-jē) *n.* **1.** The highest or farthest point; climax. **2.** The point farthest from the earth in the orbit of the moon or a satellite.

Lesson 28

con·fron·ta·tion (kŏn′frŭn-tā′shən) *n.* **1.** A conflict involving opinions, ideas, or armed forces. **2.** A face-to-face meeting. -**con′fron·ta′tion·al,** *adj.*

Lesson 28

cull (kŭl) *v.* **1.** To pick out, select. **2.** To choose and gather.

Lesson 28

ex·alt (ĭg-zôlt′) *v.* **1.** To raise in status, position, dignity, etc. **2.** To praise; glorify; extol.

Lesson 28

im·plau·si·ble (ĭm-plô′zə-bəl) *adj.* Difficult to believe; not likely. -**im·plau′si·bil′i·ty,** *n.* -**im·plau′si·bly,** *adv.*

Lesson 30 repellent	Lesson 30 viable	Lesson 30 victual	Lesson 30 vitality	Lesson 30 vivacious
Lesson 30 compulsory	Lesson 30 convivial	Lesson 30 dispel	Lesson 30 impel	Lesson 30 pulsate
Lesson 29 malleable	Lesson 29 metamorphosis	Lesson 29 modulate	Lesson 29 vacillate	Lesson 30 volatile
Lesson 29 capricious	Lesson 29 desultory	Lesson 29 ephemeral	Lesson 29 immutable	Lesson 29 inveterate
Lesson 28 primitive	Lesson 28 scrupulous	Lesson 28 suffuse	Lesson 28 transient	Lesson 28 vignette
Lesson 28 apogee	Lesson 28 confrontation	Lesson 28 cull	Lesson 28 exalt	Lesson 28 implausible

Lesson 33

pol·i·tic
(pŏl′ĭ-tĭk) *adj.* Marked by or showing good judgment, prudence, and shrewdness. **-pol′i·tic·ly,** *adv.*

Lesson 33

po·li·ti·co
(pə-lĭt′ĭ-kō′) *n., pl.* **-cos.** A politician.

Lesson 33

ur·ban
(ûr′bən) *adj.* Of, relating to, located in, or characteristic of a city or city life.

Lesson 33

ur·bane
(ûr-bān′) *adj.* **-ban·er,** **-ban·est.** Polite, refined, and courteous in a polished way.

Lesson 33

ur·ban·ite
(ûr′bə-nīt′) *n.* A person who lives in a city.

Lesson 33

cos·mo·pol·i·tan
(kŏz′mə-pŏl′ĭ-tn) *adj.* **1.** Belonging to the whole world. **2.** Sophisticated enough to be at home in all parts of the world; cultured.

Lesson 33

ge·o·pol·i·tics
(jē′ō-pŏl′ĭ-tĭks) *n.* The study of the influence of geography on the politics, power, or foreign policy of a nation. **-ge′o·po·lit′i·cal,** *adj.*

Lesson 33

im·po·li·tic
(ĭm-pŏl′ĭ-tĭk) *adj.* Not showing good judgment; unwise. **-im·pol′i·tic·ly,** *adv.*

Lesson 33

meg·a·lop·o·lis
(mĕg′ə-lŏp′ə-lĭs) *n.* A large, densely populated area made up of several adjoining cities.

Lesson 33

met·ro·pol·i·tan
(mĕt′rə-pŏl′ĭ-tən) *adj.* **1.** Relating to, resembling, or belonging to a major city. **2.** Consisting of a large city and its surrounding suburbs.

Lesson 32

in·hib·it
(ĭn-hĭb′ĭt) *v.* To hold back; hinder; restrain. **-in·hib′i·tive,** *adj.*

Lesson 32

ne·o·phyte
(nē′ə-fīt′) *n.* A beginner; novice.

Lesson 32

pre·cip·i·tate
(prĭ-sĭp′ĭ-tāt′) *v.* **-tat·ed,** **-tat·ing.** To cause to happen before needed, desired, or expected; bring on.

Lesson 32

pro·cras·ti·nate
(prō-krăs′tə-nāt′, prə-) *v.* **-nat·ed,** **-nat·ing.** To put off doing something until a future time; postpone. **-pro·cras′ti·na′tion,** *n.*

Lesson 32

thwart
(thwôrt) *v.* To prevent or obstruct from doing or succeeding; frustrate.

Lesson 32

a·bate
(ə-bāt′) *v.* **a·bat·ed, a·bat·ing.** To lessen in amount, force, degree, or intensity.

Lesson 32

de·but
(dā-byoō′, dā′byoō′) *n.* **1.** A first public appearance. **2.** The beginning of a course of action.

Lesson 32

en·cum·ber
(ĕn-kŭm′bər) *v.* **1.** To hinder or hold back the action or motion of. **2.** To burden. **-en·cum′brance,** *n.*

Lesson 32

fet·ter
(fĕt′ər) *v.* To restrain; confine; hold in check. *-n.* **1.** A shackle used for restraint. **2.** Anything that restrains.

Lesson 32

im·pede
(ĭm-pēd′) *v.* **-ped·ed,** **-ped·ing.** To hinder or obstruct the progress of.

Lesson 31

plac·id
(plăs′ĭd) *adj.* Calm; quiet; peaceful. **-pla·cid′i·ty, plac′id·ness,** *n.* **-plac′id·ly,** *adv.*

Lesson 31

pro·cure
(prō-kyŏŏr′, prə-) *v.* **-cured, -cur·ing.** To get or obtain, especially with effort. **-pro·cure′ment,** *n.*

Lesson 31

rel·ic
(rĕl′ĭk) *n.* **1.** Something from the past that has survived the passage of time and is often of historic interest. **2.** A souvenir; memento.

Lesson 31

re·lin·quish
(rĭ-lĭng′kwĭsh) *v.* **1.** To give up control of; surrender. **2.** To give up; abandon.

Lesson 31

sal·vage
(săl′vĭj) *v.* **-vaged, -vag·ing.** To save from loss or destruction. *-n.* **1.** The saving of property from destruction. **2.** The property that is saved.

Lesson 31

bul·wark
(bŏŏl′wərk, -wôrk′, bŭl′-) *n.* A means of defense or protection; safeguard.

Lesson 31

ca·lam·i·ty
(kə-lăm′ĭ-tē) *n., pl.* **-ties. 1.** A great misfortune; disaster. **2.** A time of suffering.

Lesson 31

dis·perse
(dĭ-spûrs′) *v.* **-persed, -pers·ing.** To break up, drive off, or scatter in different directions.

Lesson 31

lad·en
(lād′n) *v.* A past participle of **lade.** *-adj.* **1.** Loaded. **2.** Burdened; afflicted.

Lesson 31

per·ni·cious
(pər-nĭsh′əs) *adj.* Causing great harm, injury, or destruction. **-per·ni′cious·ly,** *adv.* **-per·ni′cious·ness,** *n.*

Lesson 33 politic	Lesson 33 cosmopolitan	Lesson 32 inhibit	Lesson 32 placid	Lesson 31 bulwark
Lesson 33 politico	Lesson 33 geopolitics	Lesson 32 neophyte	Lesson 32 procure	Lesson 31 calamity
Lesson 33 urban	Lesson 33 impolitic	Lesson 32 precipiate	Lesson 32 debut	Lesson 31 relic
Lesson 33 urbane	Lesson 33 megalopolis	Lesson 32 procrastinate	Lesson 32 encumber	Lesson 31 relinquish
Lesson 33 urbanite	Lesson 33 metropolitan	Lesson 32 thwart	Lesson 32 impede	Lesson 31 salvage
				Lesson 31 pernicious

Lesson 31 disperse
Lesson 31 laden

Lesson 36

gen·e·sis (jĕn´ĭ-sĭs) *n., pl.* **-ses** (-sēz´). The coming into being of something; beginning; origin.

Lesson 36

genre (zhän´rə) *n.* A particular type, kind, or class, especially in literature or art.

Lesson 36

het·er·o·ge·ne·ous (hĕt´ər-ə-jē´nē-əs, -jēn´yəs) *adj.* **1.** Differing in kind; dissimilar. **2.** Composed of unlike parts or elements.

Lesson 36

pri·mo·gen·i·ture (prī´mō-jĕn´ĭ-chŏŏr´) *n.* **1.** The state of being the first-born child. **2.** The right of the eldest son to inherit his family's entire estate.

Lesson 36

prog·e·ny (prŏj´ə-nē) *n., pl.* **-nies.** Children, offspring, or descendants considered as a group.

Lesson 36

con·gen·ial (kən-jēn´yəl) *adj.* **1.** Having similar tastes, temperament, or habits. **2.** Friendly and sociable. **-con·ge´ni·al·i·ty,** *n.*

Lesson 36

con·gen·i·tal (kən-jĕn´ĭ-tl) *adj.* Existing at birth; innate. **-con·gen´i·tal·ly,** *adv.*

Lesson 36

de·gen·er·ate (dĭ-jĕn´ə-rāt´) *v.* **-at·ed, -at·ing.** To worsen in quality or character; deteriorate. *adj.* (dĭ-jĕn´ər-ĭt) Having sunk to a lower state.

Lesson 36

gen·der (jĕn´dər) *n.* **1.** Category such as masculine, feminine, and neuter, into which certain words are placed. **2.** Sexual identity.

Lesson 36

ge·ner·ic (jə-nĕr´ĭk) *adj.* Relating to or applied to a whole group or class; general – A product that is sold without a brand name or trademark.

Lesson 35

fab·ri·cate (făb´rĭ-kāt´) *v.* **-cat·ed, -cat·ing.** **1.** To make up (a story, lie, etc.); invent. **2.** To manufacture; construct. **-fab´ri·ca´tion,** *n.*

Lesson 35

feign (fān) *v.* **1.** To make a false appearance of; pretend. **2.** To make believe. **3.** To make up; fabricate.

Lesson 35

pro·bi·ty (prō´bĭ-tē) *n.* Integrity; honesty; uprightness.

Lesson 35

ve·rac·i·ty (və-răs´ĭ-tē) *n., pl.* **-ties.** **1.** Truthfulness; honesty. **2.** Accuracy; correctness.

Lesson 35

ver·i·ta·ble (vĕr´ĭ-tə-bəl) *adj.* True; actual; unquestionable. **-ver·i·ta·ble·ness,** *n.* **-ver·i·ta·bly,** *adv.*

Lesson 35

ar·ti·fice (är´tə-fĭs) *n.* **1.** A clever trick. **2.** Deception; trickery.

Lesson 35

be·guile (bĭ-gīl´) *v.* **-guiled, -guil·ing.** **1.** To mislead; deceive. **2.** To amuse, delight, or charm. **-be·guile´ment,** *n.*

Lesson 35

be·lie (bĭ-lī´) *v.* **-lied, -ly·ing.** **1.** To misrepresent; disguise. **2.** To show to be false; contradict.

Lesson 35

bo·na fide (bō´nə fīd´, fī´dē, bŏn´ə) *adj.* **1.** Genuine; real. **2.** In good faith.

Lesson 35

chi·can·er·y (shĭ-kā´nə-rē, chĭ-) *n., pl.* **-ies.** **1.** Deception; trickery. **2.** A trick.

Lesson 34

gran·deur (grăn´jər, -jŏŏr´) *n.* Magnificence; splendor.

Lesson 34

im·part (ĭm-pärt´) *v.* **1.** To make known. **2.** To give; bestow.

Lesson 34

phe·nom·e·non (fĭ-nŏm´ə-nŏn´, -nən) *n., pl.* **-na** (nə). **1.** A fact, event, or circumstance that is perceptible or observed. **2.** An unusual occurrence.

Lesson 34

piv·ot·al (pĭv´ə-tl) *adj.* Of vital importance; crucial. **-piv´ot·al·ly,** *adv.*

Lesson 34

sal·u·tar·y (săl´yə-tĕr´ē) *adj.* **1.** Beneficial. **2.** Healthful. **-sal´u·tar´i·ly,** *adv.*

Lesson 34

ac·ces·si·ble (ăk-sĕs´ə-bəl) *adj.* **1.** Easily reached, entered, or approached. **2.** Easily obtained; attainable. **-ac·ces´si·bil´i·ty,** *n.* **-ac·ces´si·bly,** *adv.*

Lesson 34

de·com·pose (dē´kəm-pōz´) *v.* **-posed, -pos·ing.** **1.** To break up into basic parts or elements. **2.** To decay; rot. **-de´com·pos´a·ble,** *adj.*

Lesson 34

de·rive (dĭ-rīv´) *v.* **-rived, -riv·ing.** To get or receive from a source. **-de·riv´a·ble,** *adj.* **-de·riv´er,** *n.*

Lesson 34

e·lon·gate (ĭ-lông´gāt´, ĭ-lông´-) *v.* **-gat·ed, -gat·ing.** To make longer; lengthen. **-e·lon´ga´tion,** *n.*

Lesson 34

en·dow (ĕn-dou´) *v.* **1.** To provide with an ability, talent, quality, etc. **2.** To give money or property to.

Lesson 36 genesis	Lesson 36 congenial	Lesson 35 fabricate	Lesson 35 artifice	Lesson 34 grandeur	Lesson 34 accessible
Lesson 36 genre	Lesson 36 congenital	Lesson 35 feign	Lesson 35 beguile	Lesson 34 impart	Lesson 34 decompose
Lesson 36 heterogeneous	Lesson 36 degenerate	Lesson 35 probity	Lesson 35 belie	Lesson 34 phenomenon	Lesson 34 derive
Lesson 36 primogeniture	Lesson 36 gender	Lesson 35 veracity	Lesson 35 bona fide	Lesson 34 pivotal	Lesson 34 elongate
Lesson 36 progeny	Lesson 36 generic	Lesson 35 veritable	Lesson 35 chicanery	Lesson 34 salutary	Lesson 34 endow

Word	Lesson	Word	Lesson	Word	Lesson
a cappella	20	claimant	21	effluent	12
abate	32	clairvoyant	27	egocentric	2
abjure	6	clamorous	21	egregious	3
abstract	20	coalesce	14	élan	11
accessible	34	colloquium	18	elocution	18
accost	13	commissary	16	elongate	34
acquiesce	13	compulsory	30	embody	1
acrimonious	17	conciliatory	5	embolden	13
adjudicate	6	condescending	2	emulate	10
adjunct	3	confluence	12	encumber	32
adroit	1	confrontation	28	endemic	6
adulterate	14	congenial	36	endow	34
adverse	8	congenital	36	enjoin	3
advocate	25	congregate	3	ensemble	9
aesthetic	20	conjure	6	entente	5
aggregate	3	consternation	16	ephemeral	29
agrarian	16	consulate	5	equivocate	21
akin	22	contemptuous	2	esprit de corps	11
amalgamate	14	contradict	18	eulogize	15
ameliorate	16	convivial	30	euphemism	15
amortize	24	correlate	14	euphoria	15
apogee	28	cosmopolitan	33	euthanasia	15
appease	5	coup d'état	11	evocative	21
appendectomy	15	covert	4	exalt	28
arable	25	critique	17	excise	16
arbitration	5	crucial	19	expiration	9
arcane	4	cuisine	7	expunge	26
archives	4	cull	28	extant	13
arrogant	2	debut	32	fabricate	35
artifice	35	decadence	26	facility	4
aspersion	17	decimate	26	faux pas	11
aspirant	9	declaim	21	feign	35
aspire	10	decompose	34	fetter	32
assault	7	defame	17	flounder	8
assimilate	9	degenerate	36	fluctuate	12
attaché	5	demagogue	6	fluent	12
au contraire	11	demographics	6	foible	1
augur	7	dense	10	founder	8
avant-garde	20	depredate	26	fugitive	1
avarice	23	deride	17	gambol	16
averse	8	derive	34	gender	36
avocation	21	desultory	29	generic	36
beguile	35	dictate	18	genesis	36
belie	35	dictum	18	genre	36
bevy	7	diffuse	14	genuflect	12
bona fide	35	dispatch	4	geopolitics	33
bulwark	31	dispel	30	gluttonous	23
calamity	31	disperse	31	gossamer	7
capricious	29	disseminate	14	grandeur	34
careen	7	dissonance	20	gregarious	3
carnage	27	dulcet	20	grotesque	10
carnal	27	duress	13	haughty	2
carnivore	27	dynamic	19	heresy	19
cataclysm	26	ebullient	2	heterogeneous	36
cavalier	2	eccentric	15	heyday	25
censure	17	eclectic	15	hone	4
chicanery	35	eclipse	15	immortalize	24
circumlocution	18	ecstatic	15	immutable	29
circumscribe	4	edict	18	impart	34
		edifice	25	impeach	17

Word	Lesson	Word	Lesson	Word	Lesson
impede	32	neophyte	32	reclamation	21
impel	30	notorious	25	reconcile	10
implausible	28	nouveau riche	11	redress	13
impolitic	33	noxious	7	reflex	12
improvise	27	nuance	1	reincarnation	27
incarnate	27	nutriment	25	relic	31
inchoate	22	obliterate	26	relinquish	31
incredulous	4	obsess	23	remonstrate	17
indelible	22	obsolete	25	remorse	24
inextricably	10	obviate	13	repellent	30
inflexible	12	orient	19	repertoire	1
influx	12	overt	10	replete	23
ingenious	8	palatable	7	rigorous	16
ingenuous	8	palette	19	salutary	34
inhibit	32	par excellence	11	salvage	31
injunction	3	parsimony	23	savoir-faire	11
innate	19	periphery	14	scrupulous	28
innuendo	17	perjure	6	segregate	3
inspiration	9	permeate	14	semblance	9
intemperate	23	pernicious	31	simile	9
interdict	18	perpetuate	25	simulate	9
interpolate	26	persecute	8	stagnate	26
intimidate	25	pervasive	14	stark	1
intrinsic	10	phenomenon	34	steadfast	22
inundate	23	pidgin	19	subtle	19
inveterate	29	pivotal	34	succulent	16
invidious	27	placate	5	suffuse	28
inviolable	13	placid	31	superfluous	12
iridescent	7	plumb	22	surmount	4
irrepressible	1	politic	33	surrealistic	20
irrevocable	21	politico	33	tandem	7
judicious	6	polyglot	4	tawny	16
juncture	3	pompous	2	tête-à-tête	11
junta	3	postmortem	24	thwart	32
jurisdiction	6	precede	8	transfigure	22
jurisprudence	6	precipitate	32	transient	28
keen	1	predilection	25	transpire	9
laden	31	primitive	28	unprecedented	10
laissez faire	11	primogeniture	36	unpretentious	2
legacy	1	pristine	22	unwary	22
libretto	20	probity	35	upbraid	17
ligature	14	proceed	8	urban	33
linguist	19	proclamation	21	urbane	33
loquacious	18	proclivity	19	urbanite	33
malediction	18	procrastinate	32	vacillate	29
malleable	29	procure	31	variable	22
mastectomy	15	prodigal	23	veracity	35
megalopolis	33	profligate	23	verisimilitude	9
mellifluous	12	progeny	36	veritable	35
metamorphosis	29	propitious	5	viable	30
metropolitan	33	prosecute	8	victual	30
modulate	29	protocol	5	vie	22
mollify	13	providence	27	vignette	28
morbid	24	provocation	13	visage	27
mordant	24	proxy	5	vitality	30
moribund	24	prudent	16	vivacious	30
mortgage	24	pulsate	30	volatile	29
mortify	24	putrefaction	26	vouch	21
mortuary	24	rail	10	wane	26
motif	20	rapacity	23	waspish	2